W... ...ENTS WITH:

* BIZARRE STORIES about wacky crimes like the man who stole George Washington's wallet from a Trenton, New Jersey, museum, but later returned it because he couldn't use the $1.66 colonial money inside!

* FUN FACTS about everything from the "Best and Worst Foods" to the cases that get the biggest settlements in court to the most popular TV shows of the past four decades!

* HYSTERICAL CELEBRITY TRIVIA like the real names of such celebrities as Jodie Foster (Alicia Christian Foster) or Stefanie Powers (Stefania Zofia Federkiewicz) or Larry King (Larry Zeigler)!

* AND HUNDREDS OF OTHER ENTERTAINING TIDBITS DESIGNED TO HELP YOU GET THROUGH THAT "SPECIAL TIME" EACH DAY!

Julius Alvin's

BATHROOM BOOK

ZEBRA BOOKS
KENSINGTON PUBLISHING CORP.

ZEBRA BOOKS are published by

Kensington Publishing Corp.
475 Park Avenue South
New York, NY 10016

First Printing: September, 1993

Printed in the United States of America

To my father, Bill, for instilling in me this sacred family tradition, and to Ryan, a budding genius, who has the potential to be the most talented bathroom reader of all.

TABLE OF CONTENTS

One

Crime and Punishment

The Klutzy Criminal Department

Such esoteric criminal pursuits as jewel thefts may attract evil geniuses, but your common everyday burglaries are not committed by mental giants, just dumb criminals.

* Gregg Moore of Skiatook, Oklahoma, burglarized a house to steal sports equipment, including some hunting arrows. But on his way out, he apparently tripped on the stairs, fell on one of the arrows he was carrying, and killed himself.

* The cardinal rule of burglary is to get in, get the loot, and get out fast. The rule was broken by a burglar in Los Angeles, who decided to stay around to eat a sandwich and watch a little TV. Unfortunately, the house was unoccupied because it had just been professionally fumigated. The toxic fumes killed the burglar before he finished his snack.

* A New York City criminal klutz tried to burglarize an apartment by prying open the front door with a crowbar. He got it open far enough to get his head in, but he couldn't get it back out. When the apartment dweller returned home, he found the burglar dead, his head still stuck in the door.

* Another champion klutz was a seventeen-year-old Crescent, Iowa, man who used a gun to hold up a convenience store, then shot himself in the thigh as he walked out with the loot.

* A pair of would-be thieves smashed a Burdines department store window in Miami Beach, Florida; grabbed all the clothing on display; tossed it into the back seat of their car; then sped away. However, in their haste, the driver lost control and crashed the car. A few minutes later, the bandits watched helplessly as a crowd of seventy-five people looted the stolen clothes from their car.

* The idea, you see, is to break in, take the merchan-

dise, then steal away quietly and unobtrusively. Evidently, a forty-year-old Huntington, Indiana man didn't get the hang of planning a quiet getaway. After allegedly entering a local beer distributor's warehouse, the man imbibed a few bottles, loaded up a forklift with more than thirty cases, climbed into the driver's seat, and headed for home. Evidently, he hadn't mastered the art of handling the vehicle, because his route was strewn with dumped and broken cases. Of course, people who spotted this master criminal called the cops, who hauled him in. By the way, Huntington is the hometown of a more famous genius — Dan Quayle.

* A Burbank, California woman woke up one morning to the familiar presence of a man sleeping next to her. Then she realized that her husband was out of town on business. She crept out of bed, grabbed her infant daughter, and called the cops. Turned out the man was a drunk who had wandered in the house, stripped off his clothes, and climbed into the king-size bed to sleep it off.

* "George Washington's Mugged" was the headline. That's right, someone picked the Father of our Country's wallet from a display case at the Old Barracks Museum in Trenton, New Jersey. Fortunately, the wallet was anonymously returned three weeks later. The less-than-brilliant thief may have discovered that the $1.66 in colonial money inside couldn't buy crack.

* Two less-than-brilliant Syracuse, New York men broke into the home of an attorney and were evidently having such a good time that they snapped each other's pictures as they collected loot. The cops later recovered the camera . . . with the film still inside. The attorney had it developed and turned the conclusive evidence over to the police.

Bizarre Bank Robberies

Ever thought about robbing a bank? If you do, you don't want to imitate the would-be John Dillingers in the following true stories:

* A man wearing sunglasses and carrying a cane handed a note to a Vallejo, California, bank teller that read, "I have a bomb, so give me your money or the bomb goes off." The teller handed over $105. Then the robber had one more request—he asked the teller to lead him to the door because he was blind. She refused, and by the time the robber got to the door, the cops were waiting. Hopefully, he'll use his jail time to rethink his career plans.

* A man who robbed the Key Bank in Syracuse, New York, got away, but made just one tiny, little mistake: He left an envelope containing his wife's car loan papers at the teller's window.

* A twenty-seven-year-old man walked into an Oakland, California, savings and loan; pointed a gun at the teller; extorted a stack of bills; then stuffed the bills in the front of his pants. Unfortunately for him, the stack of bills was booby-trapped. The subsequent explosion sent him to the hospital with badly burned and brightly dyed genitals.

* A forty-nine-year-old man walked into a Brooklyn, New York, bank, handed the teller a threatening note, and walked out with $2,100. He wasn't more than a few steps out the door when a mugger stuck a gun in his back and took off with all the loot. Then the cops arrived and arrested him for bank robbery.

Bad Luck

Sometimes crime doesn't pay because bad guys are subject to the same rotten luck that occasionally afflicts all of us:

* Growing marijuana is so widespread in some areas that growers brag that their chances of getting caught are about the same as their chances of being struck by lightning. If that's true, then the odds caught up with a forty-seven-year-old resident of Howard, Wisconsin. Lightning started a fire in the man's home, igniting about eight marijuana plants growing in the basement. Firefighters recognized the aroma and

called in the cops.

* A shoplifter fled from a Baltimore store with two security guards in hot pursuit. He spotted a man sitting in a car with the engine running, hopped in the passenger's seat, and asked, "Can you get me out of here quick? Someone's chasing me."

"Sure," the driver said.

"Where are you going?" the hitchhiker asked.

"The police station," replied the driver—a Baltimore police officer assigned to cruise the parking lot in an unmarked car.

* A thirty-eight-year-old St. Louis man was hungry after a long night of imbibing at his local tavern. He got into his car, drove until he spotted a drive-through window that looked like a Burger King, and barked his order for a burger and fries into the intercom. To his surprise, the guy at the other end of the intercom was the booking clerk for the local police station. The cops soon had it their way, tossing the guy into the slammer for drunk driving.

* A twenty-year-old Dallas, Texas, man, facing up to ten years in jail for stamp theft, offered to trade a $7,900 restitution check instead of jail. There was only one small problem—the $7,900 check was forged. He now faces another ten-year sentence for forgery.

* A Pierre, South Dakota, man evidently was filled to

the gills with good cheer but was looking for more. So he wandered through the doors of what he thought was another saloon and asked the friendly face behind the bar for a drink. He'd made just one little mistake—the "saloon" was the police station and the guy behind the "bar" was the dispatcher.

* For sheer, dangerous stupidity it would be hard to top a twenty-eight-year-old nightclub owner from Staten Island, New York. And what did this Einstein-opposite do? He was carrying on an affair with the wife of Alphonse "Ally Boy" Persico, jailed son of Carmine Persico, boss of New York's Columbo crime family. Now, what do you think happened to a guy going out with the wife of a Mafia chieftain? You're right—a hail of bullets cut him down as he sat in his car outside his apartment building.

When the Good Guys Are Bad Guys

No one's a stronger supporter of law enforcement than Julius Alvin, but sometimes cops get a little carried away. Following are some examples:

* Overzealous isn't a strong enough word to describe two Hayward, California, police officers who mistook a blind man's cane for a martial arts weapon. David St. John, being blind, couldn't see that the two men demanding that he empty his pockets were wear-

ing police uniforms. So he assumed he was being mugged and he resisted. The cops responded by beating him with their nightsticks.

* In Ridge Manor, Florida, a curly-haired, little, three-year-old boy toddled onto a neighbor's lawn, playfully pulled up some flamingo lawn ornaments, then dropped them in the driveway. The outraged neighbor, evidently not a child lover, called police. A sheriff's deputy promptly arrived and dealt with the situation by arresting the toddler and charging him with criminal mischief. The cop placed the lad under house arrest and called state social workers.

Well, the diaper filling really hit the fan when the story appeared in the newspaper. The charges were dropped, and the deputy and his supervisor were suspended.

* Dodge City, Kansas, has a long and storied history of famous law enforcers. Their ranks will not be joined by a nineteen-year-old jail guard who was arrested for letting an inmate out, then driving him to a sexual rendezvous with his fifteen-year-old girlfriend.

* An Anchorage, Alaska, man was acquitted on charges of illegal salmon fishing after chagrined prosecutors admitted in court that someone had eaten all the evidence.

* Police in Boynton Beach, Florida, came under fire after the surfacing of a video tape of a camping trip

that showed police officers drunk, naked, and pretending to have sex with a man in a rabbit costume. The tape also showed six officers beating and shooting a black mannequin with "nigger" written on it. The police union said there was nothing racist on the tape.

* A thirty-six-year-old female bus driver was at the wheel of a vehicle holding forty suburban Baltimore sixth graders in the loading zone of the Maryland Science Center when a policewoman ordered her to move. She refused. The policewoman yanked this obviously hardened criminal out of the van, arrested her, stripsearched her, and tossed her in jail. The mayor of Baltimore later apologized.

* A Riverside, California, woman was raped and beaten by an intruder when police refused to respond to her home intruder alarm. The reason: The woman still owed the $25 alarm permit fee required by police. After the incident, the policy was rescinded.

* Despite strong protests, Arizona prison officials refuse to change their policy of bringing inmates to their execution wearing nothing but an adult diaper. Prison officials argue cyanide gas used in the gas chamber could cling to the clothing of the deceased, endangering those removing the body. Opponents argue that California and Mississippi convicts are removed from the gas chamber fully dressed without incident.

* "What he does on his own time is up to him." — The Bexar County, Texas, Sheriff, on a deputy charged with exposing himself to a child while off-duty.

* A Bedford, Pennsylvania, magistrate resigned after he admitted promising leniency to a male defendant if he could shampoo the man's hair. Prosecutors in the case, in which the magistrate pleaded guilty to official oppression, said the magistrate rubbed his body against people he shampooed, giving him sexual stimulation.

* The Super 8 Motel chain, evidently figuring to save a few dollars, set up a credit card reservation program that employed prisoners at the Springfield Correctional Facility in Yankton, South Dakota. Guess what? The prisoners stole so many credit card numbers the program had to be shut down.

America's Most Vicious

Did your mother ever tell you that there's some good in everybody? If she did, have her review the stories of these nasty characters:

* A twenty-five-year-old man, angry after an argument with his twenty-eight-year-old male roommate and lover, waited until his boyfriend fell asleep, took

out a hunting bow, and fired into the sleeper's skull. The arrow entered the back of the head and penetrated so deep that it popped out the forehead. He was stringing another arrow for a second shot when the victim miraculously awoke and called the police. After a two-hour operation to remove the arrow, the survivor commented, "This is so bizarre."

* A thirty-five-year-old Pompano Beach, Florida, man was given the heave-ho by his girlfriend. Evidently, that made him more than a little mad, for he allegedly broke into her house, killed her pet birds, stole her cat, and stomped her daughter's bunny to death. The cops charged him with theft and cruelty to animals. We haven't been able to confirm reports that Saddam Hussein wants to name this guy Minister of Defense.

* Most of us have used creative tactics to wheedle money out of Mom or Dad. But a twenty-two-year-old Raleigh, North Carolina, man decided on the direct approach. He grabbed a knife from the kitchen, held it to his mother's throat, took her to an automatic teller machine, and forced her to withdraw $20. Then he brought her back home, figuring she'd forget the whole thing. *Not!* She called the police.

* A thirty-five-year-old Milwaukee, Wisconsin, man allegedly flew into a rage after he and his girlfriend spent New Year's Eve watching the vampire movie, *Son of Darkness: To Die for II*. Police said the would-

be Dracula threw knives around the apartment, cut his girlfriend's chest and ear with a broken beer bottle, then tried to drink blood from her wounds.

* A fourteen-year-old Los Angeles girl allegedly resented her father's interference in her romance with a seventeen-year-old boyfriend. She wrote in her diary, "We have a plan . . . we' re going to shoot him, burn him, then bury him. . . . We have everything planned really good!" Six days later, the father was drugged with sleeping pills, shot once in the head, and his body was then burned. The fourteen-year-old girl was arrested. Her boyfriend and a sixteen-year-old girlfriend admitted to participating in the killing, according to an affidavit released by police.

* Some people just can't resist showing off their collections. However, that can be a problem if your collection is a garbage bag full of human organs. A twenty-three-year-old Costa Mesa, California, woman was arrested for murder after she showed such a bag to a male friend, who tipped police. Parts of an entire dismembered male body were found in the woman's apartment.

* A twenty-seven-year-old Houston woman was arrested after the eleven-month-old baby she was sitting for died. The reason for the tot's demise: the sitter allegedly stuffed paper towels down his throat to keep him from crying.

* A lot of professional food critics can be difficult to please, but none are quite as demanding as a sixty-two-year-old Wichita, Kansas, man. One Saturday night, he told his sixty-one-year-old girlfriend that he'd shoot her if dinner wasn't good. Evidently, the fried chicken and rice didn't pass inspection, because he allegedly got up from the dinner table, got his gun, and made good on his threat.

* Fortunately for forty-six-year-old Richard Leno of Salem, Massachusetts, it was 1992, not 1692. Otherwise, he would have been burned at the stake after he was convicted of larceny and perjury for using witchcraft to bilk an heiress out of $500,000. Among Leno's bizarre deeds was branding the heiress's breast to show his dominance over her.

* A Washington, D.C., man was a passenger in a car riding down Interstate 295 one night when he announced he "felt like killing someone." He rolled down the window, pointed his gun, and shot to death a thirty-six-year-old woman riding with her husband in a passing car.

* A Santa Ana, California, woman became enraged when her husband, a cancer sufferer, ate a chocolate Easter bunny that she had her eye on. So she allegedly doused him with rubbing alcohol and set him on fire.

* A ninety-year-old Durham, North Carolina, woman was killed by at least forty-five blows to her

face, head, back, and chest. She suffered dozens of jagged three-inch wounds, splintered vertebrae, shattered ribs, and torn internal organs. The alleged culprit: a thirteen-year-old boy who wanted to steal her car.

* A thirty-seven-year-old male employee of a Tennessee nursing home was arrested for allegedly fondling an eighty-one-year-old female patient, who has a brain disease.

* A twenty-eight-year-old Long Beach, California woman was arrested after she allegedly took a three-year-old boy from a Los Angeles day-care center, put him in a car, then set the car on fire. The boy was burned over sixty percent of his body. The woman refused to provide any explanation for the hideous act.

* A California computer expert was arrested on charges that he murdered his wife by poisoning her eyeliner and her coffee. According to police, the sixty-three-year-old man extracted the poisonous mineral selenium from an AC/DC current-changing device, then mixed it into his wife's Revlon eyeliner. She began to die slowly and painfully. But he allegedly grew impatient, and put a lethal dose of cyanide in her coffee.

Police closed in on the man when his ex-wife presented proof that he had tried to kill her in 1972 by lacing her coffee, tea, milk, wine, and Head & Shoulders shampoo with selenium. The ex-wife suffered skin lesions, sores, and rashes, but she agreed to drop charges when the man was referred to county mental health services.

* A fifty-year-old Tampa, Florida, bridegroom got into a fight with his thirty-eight-year-old bride at their wedding reception. She heaved a plate a of macaroni salad at him. He retaliated by pulling out a .22-caliber handgun and shooting her in the stomach.

The Joan Crawford Good Parent Awards

If you think the stories about Joan Crawford beating her kids with clothes hangers in *Mommie Dearest* were strong stuff, check out the parents described below:

* A Leavenworth, Kansas, couple was arrested on charges of felony murder and child abuse after the body of their four-year-old retarded son was found encased in cement in a box on the back porch of the family home.

* A Brooklyn, New York, father was baby-sitting for his twenty-two-month-old son when he allegedly grew enraged by the toddler's behavior. According to police, he took the boy to a local park, hurled him into the bushes, and left him. The boy survived a terrifying night before searchers found him the next morning.

* A Muskegon, Michigan, religious fundamentalist was convicted of murder for killing his two-year-old and fifteen-month-old sons by boiling them in a foundry ladle.

* A Lakeland, Florida, couple was convicted of murdering their two-year-old son by dunking his head in the toilet because they had trouble potty-training him.

* A twenty-three-year-old woman was arrested for allegedly putting her newborn daughter in a trash bag full of dirty cat litter and tossing the bag into the garbage.

* A thirty-seven-year old woman told police she'd been receiving mysterious telephone calls telling her that her children were replicas that she'd have to kill to get her real children back. So she beheaded her fifteen-month-old and four-month-old daughters.

* A fifty-five-year-old Long Island, New York, grandmother allegedly wanted to party on New Year's Eve, but her only companion was her five-year-old grandson. So she spent the evening dancing and feeding the tot Jell-O cubes made with vodka. Eventually, the grandson passed out and started vomiting blood. Rushed to the hospital, the lad almost died with a blood alcohol level of .252—more than twice the legal limit. Granny was arrested on charges of endangering the welfare of a minor.

* A Jacksonville, Florida, couple was arrested after their three-year-old son shot and killed their two-year-old daughter with a loaded gun left lying around the house. Police found dozens of other guns in the residence, including three more within easy reach of the children. The couple faced five years in jail — does that seem like enough?

Two

Among the Things You Probably Didn't Know . . .

How The Earth Was Formed

Our home planet, Earth, is both very, very old and relatively young. The Earth was formed about 4.5 billion years ago, a length of time incomprehensible to us, humans, who consider the few thousand years of man's recorded history to be a long time. At the same time, our sun is a relatively young star, just one-third the age of the universe. Scientists estimate that another six billion years will pass before the sun dies, taking Earth with it.

Life on Earth wouldn't have been possible if our solar system wasn't young. About 14.5 billion years ago, the universe was created when a superdense ball of matter (smaller than a baseball) exploded in what is known as the "Big Bang." About five hundred million years later, stars began to form in one huge swirl of pure hydrogen and helium to form a galaxy we call the Milky Way. Inside these massive stars, nuclear reactions fused hydrogen and helium atoms into heavier ones such as nitrogen, oxygen, silicone, iron, and, most significantly, carbon, the substance from which all life came. For eight billion years, these stars were formed, then exploded, gradually building up the concentrations of these heavier atoms.

About 4.5 billion years ago, the force of an explosion of a supernova caused a cloud of interstellar fragments to condense to the point at which the gravitational attraction between the atoms and grains of dust was stronger than the forces of dissipation. The cloud shrank and shrank until it was so dense that nuclear reactions started. At that point, the cloud became our sun.

When the sun formed, it was surrounded by clouds of leftover debris. For generations, scientists believed that Earth and the other planets condensed from smaller clouds in the same way the sun condensed. However, recent evidence proves that the Earth was formed from the billions of small, rocky bodies that circled the young sun. Because space was so crowded, these bodies frequently crashed into each other. While many of these crashes were so violent both bodies were destroyed, others were gentle enough that the bodies involved fused through gravitational attraction, forming a larger body. Although the vast majority of these planet embryos, called planetesimals, were destroyed by subsequent collisions, a handful grew bigger and bigger. One of these became Earth.

In Earth's infancy, the solar system was so filled with debris that it was bombarded daily by dozens of huge meteorites that now strike us only once in tens of thousands of years. Over a period of seventy to ninety million years, the Earth grew to its present size. At the same time, the remaining solar debris gradually flew out of our solar system or settled into a circular solar orbit that didn't threaten Earth.

How An Airplane Flies

Air travel has become so common that few of us stop and think about why something as heavy as a modern airliner can actually fly. The secret: air pressure. Now, we tend to think of air as weightless, but in truth air pressure is a powerful force—exactly how powerful you'll realize in a moment.

The main reason an airplane flies depends upon a natural fact known as the Bernoulli principle, which states that moving air has a lower pressure than the air around it. This principle is the key to the design of the wings and tail plane of an airplane. The shape, called an "aerofoil," features a flat bottom and a curved top. The air flowing over the curved top flows farther and faster than the air below, so it has less pressure. The high pressure below pushes up on the wing, a force known as "lift." This lift keeps an airplane in the air.

Why then does an airplane need a powerful engine?

For two reasons. First, the speed of an airplane has to be increased to the point where the difference in air pressure is great enough to overcome gravity. That's why large airplanes need longer runways to take off. Then, in flight, the engine has to provide sufficient power to overcome air resistance from forward motion to maintain a high enough speed to continue to provide lift.

What about helicopters? The rotors on top of the helicopter are designed so that the front edge is higher than the back. As the rotors spin, the front edge cuts into the air and forces it under the back. The more the rotors spin, the more air is pushed down and the pressure of the air under the rotors pushes the helicopter up.

The rotors also have the aerofoil shape, so that difference in air pressure provides lift when the helicopter moves in horizontally.

Flying Firsts

THE FIRST FLIGHT OFF THE GROUND

A Frenchman, Jean Pilâtre de Rozier, made the first balloon ascension on November 21, 1783, in a basket tethered to the ground. Along with the Marquis d'Arlandes, Pilâtre de Rozier made the first free flight a little more than a month later, reaching a peak altitude of five hundred feet and traveling about 5.5 miles in twenty minutes.

THE FIRST PARACHUTE JUMP

André-Jacques Garnerin dropped sixty-five hundred feet from a balloon over Monceau Park in Paris on October 22, 1797. Garnerin's chute was a twenty-three foot diameter piece of white canvas with a basket attached.

THE FIRST SUCCESSFUL HEAVIER-THAN-AIR FLIGHT

On December 17, 1903, Orville Wright crawled in a prone position between the wings of a biplane, revved up the twelve-horsepower engine, accelerated down the sand dunes of Kitty Hawk, North Carolina, then lifted into the air for a 120-foot flight lasting twelve seconds. Later that same day, his brother Wilbur stayed up fifty-nine seconds and covered 852 feet.

THE FIRST AIRPLANE MANEUVERS

On September 15, 1904, Orville Wright made the first turn with an airplane. Five days later, Wilbur Wright completed the first circle.

THE FIRST FLIGHT OVER HALF AN HOUR

Orville Wright kept his aircraft aloft for thirty-three minutes, seventeen seconds on October 4, 1905.

THE FIRST AIRPLANE FATALITY

On September 17, 1908, Lt. Thomas E. Selfridge of the U.S. Army Signal Corps was about seventy-five feet up in the air with Orville Wright when the propeller hit a bracing wire, throwing the plane out of control. Selfridge was killed and Wright seriously injured when the plane struck the ground.

THE FIRST FLIGHT FROM SHIPBOARD
Lt. Eugene Ely flew a Curtiss plane off the deck of the cruiser *U.S.S. Birmingham* on November 14, 1910. On January 18, 1911, he reversed the process by landing on the deck of the armored cruiser *Pennsylvania* in San Francisco Bay.

THE FIRST WOMAN PILOT
Baroness Raymonde de la Roche became the thirty-sixth licensed pilot in the world on March 8, 1910. American Harriet Quimby, a magazine writer, became the thirty-seventh licensed pilot and first American woman early in 1911.

THE FIRST HELICOPTER FLIGHT
Hanna Reitsch, a German pilot, flew Dr. Heinrich Focke's FW-61 in fully controlled flight on July 4, 1937.

Weather Extremes

If you think the weather gets bad in your neck of the woods, check out these world and U.S. weather extremes:

HIGHEST TEMPERATURE
The highest temperature ever recorded in the world was 136 degrees Fahrenheit in El Azizia, Libya, on Sep-

tember 13, 1922. Right behind is the U.S. record of 134 degrees Fahrenheit in Death Valley, California, on July 10, 1913. If you like your weather warm, you might want to know that the highest average annual mean temperature in the world is a scorching ninety-four degrees Fahrenheit in Dallol, Ethiopia. Highest year-round mean temperature in the U.S. is 78.2 degrees Fahrenheit in Key West, Florida.

LOWEST TEMPERATURE

When it comes to the deep freeze, no place in the world surpasses Antarctica, where the temperature on July 21, 1983, plummeted to 129 degrees below zero Fahrenheit. Lowest ever recorded in the U.S. was −80°F at Prospect Creek, Alaska, on January 23, 1971, while Rogers Pass, Montana, set a record for the lower forty-eight states when the mercury fell to −70° on January 20, 1954. If cold weather is your cup of tea, move to Barrow, Alaska, where the annual mean temperature is just 9.3 degrees Fahrenheit.

GREATEST RAINFALL

On July 4, 1956, 1.23 inches of rain fell in just one minute in Unionville, Maryland, no doubt ruining many Independence Day picnics. Holt, Missouri, had twelve inches of rain in forty-two minutes on June 22, 1947, while Alvin, Texas, was nearly washed away by forty-three inches of rain that fell in twenty-four hours on July 25-26, 1979. Cherrapunji, India, holds the all-time yearly rainfall record of 1,042 inches in August 1860 to August 1861. Wettest spot on the average goes to the 460 inches per year on Mt. Waialeale on the Hawaiian Island of Kauai.

GREATEST SNOWFALL

Silver Lake, Colorado, had an unbelievable seventy-six inches of snow in just twenty-four hours on April 14-15, 1921 — definitely a spring storm to remember. Mount Shasta Ski Bowl, California, measured 189 inches in one storm in February 1959, while Tamarack, California, recorded 390 inches in the month of January 1911. Most ever measured in one season is 1,122 inches at Paradise Ranger Station, Washington, in the winter of 1971-1972.

LONGEST HOT SPELL

Marble Bar, Australia, recorded temperatures of one hundred degrees Fahrenheit or over on 162 consecutive days running from October 30, 1923 to April 7, 1924.

LONGEST DRY SPELL

Bagdad, California, had no measurable rain for 767 days between October 3, 1912 and November 8, 1914.

LARGEST HAILSTONE

A block of ice 17.5 inches in diameter fell in Coffeyville, Kansas, on September 3, 1979.

HUGE TEMPERATURE INCREASES
AND DECREASES

In Kipp, Montana, on December 1, 1896, the temperature rose forty-nine degrees Fahrenheit in seven minutes (from −4 to 45 degrees) and eighty degrees

Fahrenheit in the next few hours. Thirty inches of snow melted in less than half that day.

At the other extreme, on January 22, 1943, the temperature in Spearfish, South Dakota, plummeted fifty-eight degrees Fahrenheit (from 54°F to −4°F) in just twenty-seven minutes.

Worst U.S. Disasters

AIRCRAFT
On May 25, 1979, an American Airlines DC-10 lost an engine while taking off from Chicago's O'Hare Airport and plunged into the ground. All 272 passengers and three people on the ground were killed.

DAM
The collapse of the St. Francis Dam created a flood that killed 450 people in Santa Paula, California, on March 12, 1928.

EARTHQUAKE
The great San Francisco earthquake of April 18, 1906, resulted in more than 500 people dead or missing.

EPIDEMIC
Spanish influenza killed an estimated five hundred thousand Americans in 1918.

EXPLOSION
On April 16-18, 1947, the French freighter *Grand-*

camp, which was carrying a cargo of ammonium nitrate, caught fire and exploded while docked in Texas City, Texas. Most of the city was destroyed, leaving 516 dead and more than three thousand injured.

FIRE
On October 8, 1871, over twelve hundred people were killed and two billion trees were destroyed by a forest fire in Peshtigo, Wisconsin.

FLOOD
More than twenty-two hundred people were killed in the Johnstown, Pennsylvania, flood of May 31, 1889.

HURRICANE
A hurricane that hit Galveston, Texas, on August 27, 1900, and lasted until September 15, 1900, caused high winds and flooding that killed more than six thousand people.

MARINE
On April 27, 1865, the boiler of the Mississippi River steamboat *Sultana* exploded near Memphis, Tennessee, killing 1,547 passengers, most of them Union soldiers recently released from Confederate prison camps.

MINE
A coal mine explosion killed 361 Monongha, West Virginia, miners on December 6, 1907.

RAILROAD

A two-train collision killed 101 passengers near Nashville, Tennessee on July 9, 1918.

TORNADO

On March 18, 1925, what is known as the "Great Tri-State Tornado" tore across parts of Missouri, Illinois, and Indiana, leaving 695 people dead.

Why Are Aristocrats Called "Blue Bloods"?

In the eighth century, Spain and some other parts of southern Europe were conquered by the Moors, a dark-skinned people from North Africa. Over a period of five centuries, they intermarried with the fair-skinned Spanish. The very thorough genetic mixing of the two peoples is obvious to anyone walking down the streets of a Spanish city today.

However, at the time of the Moorish conquest, a small group of Spanish aristocrats refused to associate with their new rulers in any way. They were allowed to retreat to the mountains of Castile in the northern part of their country. Because they abhorred their conquerors, they were anxious to emphasize their own pure heritage. One obvious way to accomplish that goal was to rigorously avoid any exposure to the sun in order to preserve the fairest possible complexion. Over the course of years, the skin of these members of the aristocracy became more and more pale. In the case of older members of this group, the skin turned nearly translucent. This allowed the veins, the blood vessels nearest the surface, to show through as bright blue. Thus these upper class Castilians came to be known as "blue bloods."

This practice of avoiding the sun spread to other European countries, especially England. Fair skin separated the upper class from the masses whose skins were tanned from laboring outdoors. The term "blue bloods" was applied to the English aristocracy and became part of the language.

Why Do We Drive On The Right Side Of The Road And The British Drive On The Left?

These practices date back long before the invention of the automobile, to the days when transportation was provided by horse-drawn or oxen-drawn vehicles. In England, the wagons were built with a driver's seat in the front. Because the brake lever was most commonly on the right side of that seat, the driver sat on the right side. When two wagons approached each other, the drivers naturally moved their vehicles to the left so they could see that their vehicles didn't collide.

In America, however, those same wagons were designed without a front seat. The driver either walked along beside the wagon holding the reins or rode on the rearmost animal. Right-handed drivers found it much easier to crack the whip over the animals if they walked or rode on the left side. When two wagons approached, these drivers naturally moved their vehicles to the right so they could insure a collision didn't take place. This common-sense safety precaution eventually became the law.

When horseless carriages were first invented, they shared the roads with a much larger number of horse-drawn vehicles. To avoid collisions, they followed the same rules of the road, which is why we drive on the right and the British on the left.

Where Did Those Phrases Come From?

Everyday we find ourselves using phrases like "his name is mud" or "I really got his goat." Ever wonder where they came from? Following are the stories behind some common phrases.

GET SOMEONE'S GOAT

A goat was often stabled with a thoroughbred horse because it had a calming effect on the high-strung racing animal. The horse would often become extremely agitated if the goat were taken away.

SOMEONE'S NAME IS MUD

After assassinating Abraham Lincoln, John Wilkes Booth fractured his leg while escaping. He stumbled into the office of Samuel Mudd, a country doctor who treated him because he had no idea what he'd done. When he learned that the president had been shot, Mudd notified authorities. Despite his innocence, he was imprisoned as a coconspirator and so vilified by an outraged public that it became a common expression of contempt to say that someone's name was "Mudd." Mudd was eventually pardoned by President Andrew Johnson, but the expression continued to be used. As the memory of the doctor faded away, "Mudd" became "mud."

LET THE CAT OUT OF THE BAG

When the Muslims invaded southern Europe in the eighth century, they banned the sale of pork, consumption of which was forbidden in their religion. However, a black market trade in pigs continued, with farmers bringing the animals to market tied up in a sack or bag. Occasionally, a dishonest farmer would substitute a cat for a pig. If the bag accidently came open, the deception would be revealed by "letting the cat out of the bag." Gradually, the term was used to mean revealing any secret.

MAD AS A HATTER

People who worked in the hat industry in the nineteenth century used mercury, which was later revealed as a powerful toxin. Persistent exposure to the substance produced uncontrollable shaking, hallucinations, and other neurological symptoms. Because of this, hatters got the reputation of being "mad."

Why Are Hurricanes Named?

In 1941, a novelist named George R. Stewart, in a book called *Storm,* created the character of a U.S.

Weather Bureau meteorologist who developed the habit of applying women's names to storms as he tracked them across the country. During World War II naming storms for women became a common practice among Air Force and Navy meteorologists. In 1950, the practice of applying women's names to tropical storms and hurricanes became official. The names were selected by meteorologists from the Weather Bureau and the Armed Services at their annual Hurricane Coordination Conference.

In 1979, men's names made the list for the first time. Today, the names on the annual lists for Atlantic storms are selected by the World Meteorological Organization Region 4 Hurricane Committee from names submitted by the countries affected by these storms.

Names chosen for the next 5 years are:

1993	1994	1995	1996	1997
Arlene	Alberto	Allison	Arthur	Ana
Bret	Beryl	Barry	Bertha	N/A
Cindy	Chris	Chantal	Cesar	Claudette
Dennis	Debby	Dean	Diana	Danny
Emily	Emesto	Eri	Edouard	Erika
Floyd	Florence	Felix	Fran	Fabian
Gert	Gordon	Gabrielle	Gustav	Grace
Harvey	Helene	Humberto	Hortense	Henry
Irene	Isaac	Iris	Isidore	Isabel
Jose	Joyce	Jerry	Josephine	Juan
Katrina	Keith	Karen	Klaus	Kata
Lenny	Leslie	Luis	Lili	Larry
Maria	Michael	Marilyn	Marco	Mindy

Nate	Nadine	Noel	Nana	Nicholas
Ophelia	Oscar	Opal	Omar	Odetta
Phillippe	Patty	Pablo	Paloma	Peter
Rita	Rafael	Roxanne	Rene	Rose
Stan	Sandy	Sebastian	Sally	Sam
Tammy	Tony	Tanya	Teddy	Teresa
Vince	Valerie	Van	Vicky	Victor
Wilma	William	Wendy	Wilfred	Wanda

Snowflakes—Are There Really No Two Alike?

In 1880, a young Vermont farmer named Wilson Bentley purchased a microscope and used it to examine a snowflake. What he saw through the eyepiece was an incredibly delicate, beautiful, six-sided structure formed from ice crystals. The sight was so breathtaking and fascinating, Bentley rigged up a camera to take a picture through the microscope.

Over the next forty years, "Snowflake" Bentley, as he came to be called, took thousands of pictures of snowflakes. Eventually, he was able to list more than eighty different categories of snowflake structure. Yet over all those years, he never found two snowflakes that were alike.

But contrary to what you've always read and heard, scientists have never found a law of nature that prohibits two snowflakes from being identical. However, each snowflake contains about 180 billion water molecules that come together in such a random way under such a variety of conditions that observing two that are identical is extremely unlikely. Researchers have found that snowflakes formed at certain temperatures are often similar in appearance: At temperatures over twenty-seven degrees Fahrenheit they are flat and hexagonal; between twenty-three and twenty-seven degrees Fahrenheit they tend to be needlelike; between eighteen degrees and twenty-three degrees Fahrenheit they tend to be hollow, prismatic columns. At lower temperatures, variety again prevails.

One characteristic of snowflakes is they are extremely good insulators. The reason: A lot of air is trapped inside the ice crystals that make up a snowflake. This insulating ability accounts for the eerie quiet that is characteristic of a snowfall. Snow cover is also a thermal insulator—during one Midwestern cold snap, the temperature on the surface of the snow was −27°F, while just seven inches below the surface the temperature was twenty-four degrees Fahrenheit. That's why Eskimos are comfortable in igloos.

Why Don't Clouds Fall From the Sky?

For centuries, men of scientific bent spent untold hours trying to figure out why clouds seemed to be immune to the forces of gravity that pulled everything, including water drops, toward the earth. Among the fanciful solutions offered to this puzzle was the theory that water in the air consisted of tiny bubbles floating upward like balloons. But it wasn't until this century that we finally learned that cloud droplets are incredibly small, less than 1/2500 of an inch in diameter. It takes more than one million cloud droplets to form an average size raindrop. You'd need to collect as many as seven billion droplets to make a tablespoon of water. Only trying to count the grains of sand on a beach is comparable to trying to calculate the incredible number of these droplets that form the average puffy cloud drifting overhead on a summer day.

Every object that falls from a high enough height, steel ball to a feather, has a terminal velocity, a point at which air pressure balances the additional pull of gravity. Because they are so small and light, cloud droplets have a terminal velocity, or maximum rate of fall, of .02 miles per hour or about two feet per minute. The slightest updraft will stop their descent as the cloud blows along with the wind. Those that do drift into warmer air evaporate quickly.

Because cloud droplets are so numerous that it takes several million of them to fill a cubic inch, you'd think that airplanes would get wet passing through clouds. The truth is that all these droplets don't add up to very much water. In a cloud, there's only a total of about one ounce of water in a space the size of the average 15' × 20' living room.

But clouds are pretty big—so if you could figure out a way to wring one out, you'd end up with a fair amount of water. To obtain a rough measurement of the total weight of water in one of those puffy cumulus clouds, scientists estimate the size of the shadow the cloud makes on the ground when the sun is directly overhead. Say the shadow measures 1/2 mile square, and assume it is as tall as it is wide. Multiplying length times width times height to get cubic feet, then dividing by .01765 ounces of water per cubic feet gives you a total of a little under a million ounces of water, or about 58,000 pounds.

What's The Difference Between . . .

KARAT AND CARAT?

No, they aren't two different spellings of the same term. Karat is a measure of the purity of gold. Pure gold equals twenty-four karats. Fourteen-karat gold contains a ratio of fourteen parts gold to ten parts alloy, or about three-fifths gold.

Carat, on the other hand, is a unit of weight used in measuring diamonds and other precious gems. One carat equals .2 grams, so a five-carat diamond weighs one gram.

CEMENT AND CONCRETE?

Cement is an ingredient of concrete. Although the term can be used for any bonding agent, it most commonly refers to a dry mixture of calcium silicate and aluminates. Concrete is made by adding cement to sand, gravel, and water.

DEMOCRACY AND REPUBLIC?

A democracy is a form of government controlled by elected representatives of the people. A republic is any form of government with no hereditary ruler or king. The United States is a democracy and a republic, while Great Britain is a democracy, but not a republic. China is a republic, but not a democracy.

DOCK, PIER, AND WHARF?

Otis Redding was wrong when he sang he was "sittin' on the dock of the bay." Why? A dock is a body of water, often man-made, in which a ship is moored, loaded or unloaded, or repaired. A dry dock is such an area that has been emptied of water.

Rather, Otis was probably sitting on a pier, which is a man-made structure running out into the water. A wharf, also man-made, is a structure that runs parallel to the shore.

HORNS AND ANTLERS?

Horns are actually part of an animal's skull. They grow slowly and are attached for life. Both sexes of such animals as cows and mountain sheep have horns.

Antlers are bony structures that grow out of an animal's head but are not attached to the skull. They grow very quickly—up to half an inch per day—but they drop off each year. Normally, only males grow antlers.

LIBEL AND SLANDER?

Both refer to false accusations that damage a person's personal and/or professional reputation. But slander refers strictly to verbal statements that are heard by one or more people. Libel refers to more long-lasting statements that are written, recorded on film or tape, or otherwise preserved.

MURDER AND HOMICIDE?

Although the words seemed to be used interchangeably on police shows, a homicide is any killing of a human being, whether it involves an illegal act or not. An accidental death, a combat fatality, even a legal execution are all homicides.

Murder, on the other hand, is a strictly illegal killing. That's why it would be more strictly accurate if police departments had murder detectives instead of homicide detectives.

RABBITS AND HARES?

No, these words aren't interchangeable — in fact, they refer to two separate species. Rabbits are smaller animals that burrow. They are born blind and hairless, and they grow up to be very social.

Hares are larger, are able to hop around after birth, and nest above the ground. Hares are generally solitary animals.

Is the distinction clear? It evidently hasn't always been. The animals we call jackrabbits are really hares, while Belgian hares are really rabbits.

What Does The Federal Government Spend Its Money On?

All of us hate paying taxes. So, when the subject of reducing the deficit comes up, our reaction is, "Cut out all that waste in government!" Of course, we don't want to cut social security benefits or Medicare or weaken our defense. We have to pay interest on the money the government has borrowed. So, we'll concentrate on cutting the waste in the other programs.

Good plan, with one major problem: The Federal

government would operate at a deficit if it didn't spend one cent on anything other than income security, national defense, interest, and health. Following is the percentage of the Federal budget spent on major programs:

1. Income security (social security, unemployment, etc.)   31.45%
2. National defense   25.40%
3. Interest on the national debt   14.11%
4. Health (Medicare, Medicaid, etc.)   11.63%
5. Education, Job Training, Social services   3.10%
6. Veteran's benefits and services   2.41%
7. Transportation   2.39%
8. Agriculture   1.78%
9. Commerce and housing   1.71%
10. Environmental protection   1.40%

Three

Where in the World?

The Seven Wonders of the World

In the days before the invention of heavy motorized equipment, raising great buildings and monuments were awe inspiring feats that often took centuries to accomplish. Word of these structures spread throughout the known world. Gradually, a list of the most famous were compiled by classical writers. This list became known as the "Seven wonders of the ancient world."

WONDER ONE: THE PYRAMIDS OF GIZA

These three pyramids built at Giza near Cairo were not only considered the greatest of all the wonders of the ancient world, but they are also the only wonder to survive today. The largest, known as the Great Pyramid, was built for Egyptian King Khufu about 800 B.C. When the Greeks listed this wonder, they corrupted the king's name to the Greek Cheops, by which the pyramid is sometimes known today.

The sides of the Great Pyramid are 755 feet long, and the structure soared 450 feet into the air. It was constructed of 2,300,000 stone blocks each weighing 2.5 tons—the combined weight of two automobiles. Each stone had to be carefully cut, then dragged up a granite ramp to its proper place—a feat of immense labor.

WONDER TWO: THE HANGING GARDENS OF BABYLON

These gardens were made up of terraces at different levels to form a pyramid shape. The terraces were covered with trees and flowers brought from all over the world, and the vegetation made them look as if they were suspended in the air. The structure was supposedly built around 600 B.C. by Nebuchadnezzar to please one of his queens, Amuhia.

WONDER THREE: MAUSOLEUM AT HALICARNASSUS

Mausolus was king of Caria, a coastal region of Asia Minor in modern-day Turkey. Upon his death in 353 B.C., his widow Queen Artemisia ordered the construction of a magnificent tomb 130 feet high with beautiful friezes on all four sides. This tomb, from which we get the modern word "mausoleum," survived until leveled by an earthquake in the fifteenth century.

WONDER FOUR: THE TEMPLE OF ARTEMIS AT EPHESUS

This temple dedicated to the goddess of chastity, childbirth, and the hunt was constructed at Ephesus on the coast of modern-day Turkey about 350 B.C. The building, which covered four times the area of the Parthenon in Athens, included 127 Ionic columns each sixty feet high. It was constructed of marble and adorned with sculpture inside and out. It was ravaged by the invading Goths in 262 A.D., and cannibalized for its building materials. A single column survives today.

WONDER FIVE: THE COLOSSUS AT RHODES

This bronze figure of the sun god Helios (Apollo) was 105 feet high, eighteen times the size of a man. It was constructed beside, not across, the harbor of the Greek city of Rhodes in 280 B.C. It was toppled by an earthquake in 224 B.C.

WONDER SIX: THE STATUE OF ZEUS AT OLYMPIA

This statue of Zeus sitting in a richly carved chair was the centerpiece of the temple in Olympia, home of the Olympic games. Carved about 480 B.C. by the sculptor Phidias, it stretched forty feet high and was adorned with gold, ivory, and precious stones. No trace remains except images on coins.

WONDER SEVEN: THE PHAROS (LIGHTHOUSE) OF ALEXANDRIA

This lighthouse, the first in the ancient world, was constructed about 250 B.C. on the island of Pharos off the important Egyptian port city of Alexandria. It stood six hundred feet high, with a top covered in bronze sheets that, like mirrors, reflected the light of the fire kept blazing day and night. This lighthouse was toppled by an earthquake in the thirteenth century.

Bridges

Somewhere in the unfathomable darkness of prehistory, one of our ancestors came up with the idea of felling a tree to span a river or gorge, saving a long walk to the nearest ford or crossing place. Human nature being what it is, someone felled a tree soon afterwards, then sat next to it charging a toll to people who wanted to cross. Customers probably paid, because bridges are, and have always been, crucial to the transportation system of a country, county, or city. New York City alone sports 1,420 bridges, without which the city would grind to a halt. Bridges can be beautiful and awe-inspiring, too, which is why bridges from the Golden Gate to the old London have been celebrated in poems, songs, novels, movies, and art.

If you have an eye for a great bridge, you'll be interested in these facts:

LONGEST BRIDGE
The Lake Pontchartrain No. 2 bridge in New Orleans, Louisiana, is 23.87 miles long. Completed in 1969, this bridge features an eight-mile stretch that is completely out of sight of land.

TALLEST BRIDGE
The towers of the Golden Gate Bridge over San Fran-

cisco Bay top off at 745 feet above the water.

HIGHEST BRIDGE

The Royal Gorge Bridge was built 1,053 feet over the Arkansas River in central Colorado. It's the highest suspension bridge above water in the world.

COSTLIEST BRIDGE

The Verrazano-Narrows Bridge which spans New York harbor to connect Staten Island with Brooklyn was completed in 1964 at a cost of $304 million.

HEAVIEST LOAD-CARRYING CAPACITY

The Hell Gate Bridge over New York City's East River can carry twenty-four thousand pounds per square foot. It was built as a railroad bridge in 1917.

What Is Our Sun and How Does It Work?

Our sun, like all other stars, is really a giant nuclear reactor in the sky. The first stars were formed about fourteen billion years ago, about a billion years after the universe began with the "big bang," an explosion of a single point of infinite density and infinite temperature. Some of the tiny particles shot forth from this explosion eventually combined to form hydrogen and helium atoms. Random dispersion caused concentrations of these atoms, which were formed into clusters by the force of gravity. Gradually, gravity drew more and more atoms into balls that became increasingly hot as they became more dense and the atoms collided more frequently. When the temperatures reached about twenty million degrees, nuclear fusion began, a process which converted hydrogen atoms into helium atoms. The pressure from this conversion balanced the force of gravity, stabilizing these balls of atoms which were now transformed into stars.

About 4.55 billion years ago, the explosion of a giant star somewhere in the universe disrupted a huge cloud of dust and gas in a part of the universe we call the Milky Way. The huge cloud broke up into a number of smaller clouds that condensed into stars. Some were twin stars that orbited each other, and a few consisted of groups of three or more stars. And one was a single star we call the "sun."

Compared to the hundreds of billions of stars in the universe, our sun is slightly below average in size. Its diameter is 865,400 miles, its surface area is approximately twelve thousand times that of Earth, and its mass is 332,000 times that of our planet.

The average distance of the sun from the Earth is about ninety-three million miles, which is used as a unit of measurement called an Astronomical Unit (A. U.). The Earth is closest to the sun in January (91.5 million miles) and farthest away in July (94.5 million miles), but these variations don't have a measurable effect on our weather. The light from the sun takes approximately eight and a half minutes to reach Earth (the speed of light is 186,000 miles per second), so that distance can also be expressed as 8.5 light minutes. By comparison, the nearest star, Alpha Centauri, is about 4.3 light years away.

While Earth revolves around the sun, the sun revolves around the center of the Milky Way at a speed of about 175 miles per second. One revolution—a solar year—

takes about 220 million earth years. Meanwhile, the whole galaxy is moving through space toward the constellation Hercules at about twelve miles per second.

It took more than two billion years for the sun's "furnace" to reach full efficiency; initially the sun gave off less than seventy-five percent of the energy that it does today. Now, with the furnaces fully stoked, the sun's internal temperature is an estimated thirty-six million degrees Fahrenheit, and the surface temperature is about eleven-thousand degrees Fahrenheit. The sun burns four million tons of hydrogen every second, producing this awesome amount of energy:

* An area of the sun's surface—the size of a postage stamp—gives off enough energy to power five-hundred sixty-watt light bulbs.
* One horsepower is the amount of energy necessary to lift thirty-three thousand pounds a distance of one foot for one minute. Each square yard of the sun emits seventy-two thousand horsepower. The sun's average total output in horsepower is five hundred followed by twenty-one zeros.

Because the sun radiates energy 360 degrees, Earth intercepts only a tiny portion—just one part in two billion. Yet that seemingly insignificant percentage amounts to five-million horsepower per square mile of Earth's surface. If the amount of the sun's energy that hits the Earth in one hour could be trapped and harnessed, it would meet the world's total annual energy needs. To replace the energy received from the sun in just one day, we would have to burn seven hundred billion tons of coal.

The amount of solar energy that reaches the Earth is just the right amount to sustain life. If the amount of sunlight was cut by just ten percent, our planet would be a frozen ball of ice.

Where Is Our Water Today?

The total volume of Earth's water is 326 million cubic miles (at more than twenty-six billion gallons per cubic mile, an incomprehensible amount). The amount of water in our biosphere (a fancy name for our environment) has neither increased nor decreased in billions of years.

However, the vast majority of that water, 97.2 percent, is salt water in the oceans. Another 2.1 percent is locked up in the ice caps. That leaves less than one percent for all the people, animals, and plants in the world. To put it in further perspective, if all the water on earth were represented by twenty-five gallons, all life would have to exist on just one teaspoon.

The distribution of our fresh water is:

	Volume (cubic miles)	%of total
All freshwater lakes	30,000	.009
All rivers	300	.0001
Antarctic ice cap	6,300,000	1.9
Arctic ice cap & glaciers	680,000	.21

Water in atmosphere	3,100	.001
Ground water within 1/2 mile of surface	1,000,000	.31
Deep ground water	1,000,000	.31
Total fresh water	10,013,400	2.7391

Fresh water in lakes and rivers would soon disappear if it weren't replenished by rain or snow. At any given time, there's only enough water in the atmosphere to drop one inch of rain over all the Earth's surface, just a ten- to twelve-day supply. Fortunately, an immense amount of water is constantly evaporating from the oceans — 104 million billion gallons, about one quarter of the oceans' total volume, evaporate every year. Most of this water falls back in the ocean. But some is blown over land, falling as rain or snow to replenish freshwater supplies. It replaces water that makes its way down streams or rivers into the ocean.

If You Want to Feel Insignificant. . . .

We humans tend to be a bit self-centered, so it's useful to gain some perspective by taking a look at our planet in relationship to the universe. Our solar system is part of the Milky Way galaxy, a cluster of about two billion stars. The Milky Way, in turn, is just one of approximately ten billion galaxies. That means, conservatively, that there are at least 20,000,000,000,000,000,000 (or

200,000 trillion) stars.

How much space do all these stars fill? To even begin to understand the dimensions of space, let's start by exploring the concept of the "light year"—that is, the distance light travels in one year. Light travels at 186,000 miles per second, or a little over eleven million miles a minute. It takes the sun's light about 7.5 minutes to travel the ninety-three million miles to earth. The nearest star is 4.225 light years, or twenty-five trillion miles away. That kind of distance is hard to comprehend—if we shrunk the universe so that the sun was just one inch in diameter, the nearest star (also one inch in diameter) would still be forty billion miles away.

The Milky Way, our galaxy, has a diameter of seventy thousand light years. The most distant object in the universe ever detected is an estimated 13,200 million light years (or seventy-eight million trillion miles) away.

And what about other planets in the universe? Astronomers have never conclusively detected any. But if you think about the vastness of the universe and the incredible number of stars, does it make sense we're alone?

How Did The States Get Their Names?

Of the fifty U.S. states, only one is named after a prominent American—see if you can guess what state that is. More than half of the rest (twenty-eight states) have names derived from Native American languages. Ten state names honored British nobility, three came from European locations, six state names have Spanish origins, and two are French. You can probably figure out that the District of Columbia honored Christopher Columbus, but you may not know that the United States was often called "Columbia" before 1800.

* ALABAMA is named after the Alabama tribe, whose name in turn means "thicket-clearers" or "vegetation-gatherers."
* ALASKA is a corruption of an Aleut word *"alaska"* and the Eskimo word *"alkshak,"* which means "great land" or "mainland."
* ARIZONA comes from the Indian word *"Arizonac,"* which means "little springs."
* ARKANSAS was taken from the name given to the Quapaw Indian tribe by other tribes.
* CALIFORNIA was the name of a mythical island in a sixteenth century Spanish romance written by Garcia Ordóñez de Montalvo — in other words, a place sort of like "Shangri-la."
* COLORADO is from the Spanish for "ruddy" or "red," and was probably applied because of the reddish soil of the plateaus.
* CONNECTICUT comes from the Indian word *"Quinnehtukqut,"* which means "beside the long tidal river."
* DELAWARE is named for the colony's first governor, Sir Thomas West, Lord De La Warr.
* FLORIDA was named by Ponce De Leon after the *Pascua Florida,* "the Easter feast of flowers."
* GEORGIA was named after King George II of England.
* HAWAII probably came either from Hawaii Loa, the discoverer of islands in Polynesian folklore, or from Hawaiki, the traditional Polynesian homeland.

* IDAHO was derived NOT from the Indian word for "potato," but from an Indian word meaning "gem of the mountains."

* ILLINOIS comes from a French butchering of the Indian word *"iliniwek,"* which means "tribe of superior men."

* INDIANA means "land of Indians." (If anyone can't figure this one out, you'd better give them detailed instructions on how to use toilet paper.)

* IOWA was derived from an Indian word meaning "The Beautiful Land."

* KANSAS was shaped from the Kansa or Kaw, "people of the south wind."

* KENTUCKY probably came from the Iroquoian word "Ken-tah-ten," which meant "land of tomorrow."

* LOUISIANA was named for Louis XIV, who was King when La Salle claimed the area for France in 1682.

* MAINE was given its designation to distinguish it from the offshore islands. The name was possibly applied to honor Henrietta Maria, Queen to Charles I of England. She owned the French province of Mayne.

* MARYLAND was also a moniker that honored Henrietta Maria, Queen to Charles I.

* MASSACHUSETTS was derived from two Indian words meaning "great mountain place."

* MICHIGAN came from two Indian words meaning "large lake," or, perhaps, "great lake."

* MINNESOTA, yet another title based on the Indian's ability to turn a phrase, was from the Dakota word *"minisota,"* which means "sky-tinted waters."

* MISSISSIPPI had its root in the Ojibwa words *"misi sipi,"* which means "great river"—the extra letters must have been added by somebody who wanted the name to

be more fun to spell.

* MISSOURI came from the word those "superior men" (the *Iliniwek*) used to refer to "owner of big canoe."

* MONTANA is the Spanish word for "mountainous."

* NEBRASKA was corrupted from an Oto Indian word meaning "flat water."

* NEVADA, which is far from flat, got its name from the Spanish word for "snowcapped sierra."

* NEW HAMPSHIRE was named after the English county of Hampshire. (How old does New Hampshire have to be before it's not considered "new" anymore?)

* NEW JERSEY got its name from Jersey, an island in the English Channel.

* NEW MEXICO was named after another Spanish colony, Paraguay — NOT!

* NEW YORK honored the Duke of York, who later became James II. Maybe they should have changed the name to New James II.

* NORTH CAROLINA was named for King Charles I of England (Carolus is Latin for Charles).

* NORTH DAKOTA came from *"Dakota,"* the Sioux word for "allies."

* OHIO was derived from the Iriquois word *"oheo,"* meaning "beautiful."

* OKLAHOMA stemmed from the Choctaw phrase *"okla humma,"* meaning "land of the red people."

* OREGON's origin is unknown, but the word was believed to have been first used as a name for what is now called the Columbia River.

* PENNSYLVANIA was not named for William Penn, founder of the Commonwealth, but for his father, Ad-

miral William Penn.

* RHODE ISLAND came from the name of an island in Narragansett Bay, which was in turn named after the Mediterranean island of Rhodes.

* SOUTH CAROLINA (see North Carolina)

* SOUTH DAKOTA (see North Dakota)

* TENNESSEE apparently came from Tenase, the name of a large Cherokee settlement.

* TEXAS was derived from the Indian word *"tavshas,"* meaning "friends."

* UTAH was named for the Ute tribe, meaning "people of the mountains."

* VERMONT came from the French *"vert mont,"* meaning "green mountain."

* VIRGINIA honored Elizabeth I, the Virgin Queen.

* WASHINGTON — Let's see if you can guess who this state was named for.

* WEST VIRGINIA (see Virginia).

* WISCONSIN came from the Ojibwa word *"wishkonsing,"* meaning "place of the bearer."

* WYOMING was derived from the Indian word *"maugh-wau-ma-wa,"* meaning "mountains and valleys alternating." The state was named for Wyoming Valley in Pennsylvania.

How Many People Are There and Where in the World Do They Live?

At the end of 1992, the world population had passed the 5.5 billion mark. Every two seconds, nine babies are born, and only three people die. The net increase is 10,600 people per hour, 254,000 per day, 1.8 million per week, 7.7 million per month, and ninety-three million per year. The equivalent of the entire current U.S. population is added every 2.5 years.

Ninety percent of the population increase occurs in developing countries, a percentage that will grow to ninety-eight percent by the year 2020. The population of many countries, such as Iran, Nigeria, and Pakistan, will more than double between 1990 and 2025 as their females give birth to an average of nearly seven babies. During the same period, the population of the United Kingdom, France, Germany, and other European countries is expected to actually fall.

Where do people live now? Of every one hundred people in the world:

* Twenty-one live in China.
* Sixteen live in India.
* Five live in the republics of the former Soviet Union.
* Five live in the United States.
* Four live in Indonesia.
* Three live in Brazil.
* Two live in Bangladesh.
* Two live in Japan.
* Two live in Mexico.
* Two live in Nigeria.
* Two live in Pakistan.

By regions of the world:

* Sixty live in Asia.
* Twelve live in Africa.
* Nine live in Europe.

* Eight live in Central and South America.
* Five live in the former Soviet Union.
* Five live in the U.S. and Canada.
* One lives in Oceania.

By the year 2025, the distribution will be:

* Fifty-eight will live in Asia.
* Eighteen will live in Africa.
* Nine will live in Central and South America.
* Six will live in Europe.
* Four will live in the U.S. and Canada.
* Four will live in the former Soviet Union.
* One will live in Oceania.

Four

Everything You Ever Wanted to Know About Death

What a Way to Go!

All of us eventually exit this life, but some people's ends are not only unfortunate, but truly bizarre:

ATTACK OF THE KILLER BEDS
Five-year-old Anthony Craddock was killed in Harlem Hospital in New York City when his electrically operated bed suddenly closed up, strangling him. To add insult to injury, the hospital first listed the cause of death as AIDS-related pneumonia.

DOUBLE WHAMMY

Evangelista Denigris of Queens, New York, was on his way home from work one night when he lost control of his car, which flipped upside down on a major parkway. Miraculously, Denigris survived. He somehow managed to crawl out of the wreckage—then was killed when a hit-and-run driver smashed into him.

PARTY ANIMALS, BEWARE!

Joe Rutherford of Memphis, Tennessee, had a few drinks while waiting to change planes in St. Louis. Evidently bored, the man spotted an electric cart, got in, and started racing around the airport. His antics caught the attention of the cops, who gave chase. Then Rutherford made a mistake—he decided to hide in a trash compactor. A few minutes later, there wasn't enough left of him to fit in a carry-on bag.

KILLER TOOTHPICKS

The *New England Journal of Medicine* reported that an autopsy revealed that a California man died of complications caused by swallowing a toothpick six months earlier. The toothpick had lodged in an abdominal artery, causing fever, chills, and bleeding. The publication also reported that toothpicks had caused 8,176 serious injuries over a four-year period, including three other deaths.

OBESITY CAN BE HAZARDOUS TO YOUR HEALTH

A forty-seven-year-old Connecticut man was killed when his five hundred-pound wife fell on him during an argument. The man allegedly had called her a "fatass ox." So she allegedly fell on her 170-pound husband, beat him with her shoe, had her son tie the man's hands, then sat on him until police arrived.

TURN REGULARLY FOR EVEN TANNING

A forty-five-year-old Chicago woman who was taking medication that made her skin more sensitive to light was roasted to death during a session in a tanning booth.

GO DIRECTLY TO JAIL, DO NOT PASS GO

A twenty-five-year-old Doylestown, Pennsylvania, man pleaded guilty to criminal homicide for shooting a friend in the chest with an arrow after an argument about Monopoly game rules.

IN THE REALLY, REALLY DUMB IDEA DEPARTMENT

A seventeen-year-old boy was woodchuck hunting with his thirty-one-year-old friend in a Potter, New York, field when he got the idea it might be fun to hide and make grunting noises like a woodchuck. You guessed it—the thirty-one-year-old man shot and killed him. No charges were filed.

HE RUBBED HIM THE WRONG WAY

A fifteen-year-old Kansas boy who squeezed his friend's head while giving him a "Dutch rub" faced murder charges. The reason: The friend died from the rub.

HE BRAGGED, HE CHOKED, HE CROAKED

A seventeen-year-old Dekalb, Mississippi, boy was

sitting in the school cafeteria discussing who could eat a sandwich the fastest. The seventeen-year-old decided to end the discussion by shoving almost all of a ham sandwich in his mouth. Instead, he ended his life, choking to death.

PLAYING LOBSTER

A twenty-four-year-old employee of the U.S. Fish and Wildlife Service was taking a steam bath with some friends near a volcanic vent in Hawaii Volcanoes National Park. As she got up to leave, she slipped, fell fifteen feet down the 2-1/2-foot hole, and was scalded to death.

MORE THAN A CLOSE SHAVE

A twenty-two-year-old Canton, Ohio, man was electrocuted while shaving with his electric razor.

SCOTCHGARD KILLS TWENTY

A fourteen-year-old Fox Lake, Illinois, boy died after sniffing the fumes from Scotchgard, an aerosol fabric protectant. Seven of his friends were hospitalized. A spokesperson for 3M, makers of Scotchgard, said the death was the twentieth attributed to its misuse over the last two years.

INSTANT FUNERAL

A twenty-five-year-old Virginia man was killed in Hamden, Connecticut, when he lost control of his car, crashed into a cemetery, and was hurled from the car into a headstone. All they had to do was toss on a couple of bouquets.

DEADLY HIDE-AND-SEEK

A four-year-old New York City boy who chose a closet as his hiding place for a game of hide-and-seek was crushed to death by the weight of the clothing on his chest.

MOWED DOWN

An eight-year-old girl sitting on the front porch of her grandmother's house in Manchester, Kentucky, was killed by a rock flung from a county highway department mowing machine.

SCENES FROM THE MAUL

A twenty-year-old college student who was collecting soil samples for a mining company in northeastern Ontario, Canada, was mauled to death by a black bear. No word on whether the bear was against exploitation of mineral rights.

OVERCONFIDENCE CAN BE FATAL

A Coupeville, Washington, man was drinking with some buddies one Saturday afternoon near the Deception Pass Bridge. The man started bragging that he'd leapt from higher elevations than the 140 feet from the bridge to the water below. Evidently looking to impress them with his actions, he shouted a cheerful "Yahoo!" and jumped. However, witnesses saw the man's body being sucked into a whirlpool in the rough, three hundred-foot-deep water. A search failed to turn up his body.

A LITTLE TO THE LEFT—SPLAT!

A Long Island man was working his very first day as a garbage collector when he had to direct the driver who was backing up the truck. Evidently, the neophyte trashman wasn't too good at hand signals, because the truck ran over him, crushing him to death.

NOTHING LIKE DYING FOR A GOOD CAUSE

A Calgary, Canada, man drowned while attempting to retrieve golf balls from a pond on the third hole of a local golf course.

TV CAN BE DANGEROUS TO A CHILD'S HEALTH

A two-year-old Hialeah, Florida, girl was climbing onto a dresser to turn on the TV when the set fell, killing her.

SLIMED

A Los Angeles husband and his nine-months-pregnant wife were sleeping in their bed when a river of mud poured in through their open window and suffocated them. The mud flow was caused by days of torrential rains.

ACCIDENT OR DIVINE RETRIBUTION

A sixteen-year-old Roxboro, North Carolina, boy was awaiting trial on charges that he killed a motorist by throwing a sixty-pound boulder off a highway bridge. He took a job at a manufacturing plant to help pay for his defense. Shortly afterwards, he died when he was electrocuted while working on the plant's roof.

BLACK DEATH

A man hopped a coal train heading east out of Denver, then fell asleep in a coal car as the train moved across the plains. Unfortunately, he didn't wake up when the train arrived to dump its load in Holcomb, Kansas. The sleeping man was killed as the car was dumped into a twenty-five-foot deep pit and three hundred tons of coal landed on top of him.

DEADLY GAME OF PIRATE

Two boys playing pirate were dueling with curtain rods on a Queens, New York, street when one boy slipped, impaling the other boy's head with his rod.

Methods Of Execution

Our modern anguish about the morality of the death penalty would seem silly to most of the people who have lived since the dawn of civilization. Cruel public executions, throughout most of history, have been viewed as the best way to insure public order — and, at the same time, provide entertainment. Even the most "civilized" of nations featured frequent executions — during the reign of Henry VIII, a whopping seventy-two thousand Englishmen were put to death.

Following are short histories of some of the most popular forms of execution.

STONING

Perhaps because this form of execution allowed audience participation, it was extremely popular dating back to the time of Moses. However, it was far from random violence. The crowd surrounded the condemned person, then the victim of the offense stepped forward and "cast the first stone." A rain of heavy stones followed, but they were carefully aimed to avoid hitting the head. The purpose was to prolong the suffering, and, ideally, the criminal died a slow death by suffocation.

CRUCIFIXION

Even though the Romans were the most famous perpetrators of this cruel form of execution, they didn't invent it. That dubious honor goes to the Phoenicians, who developed one of the first great civilizations that contributed the alphabet, among other things, to mankind's development. Because the Phoenicians widely traded throughout the Mediterranean, their favorite method of lethal punishment was also widely disseminated, not only to Rome, but to Egypt, Assyria, Persia, and Carthage as well. The Carthagenians even used it as a form of ritual sacrifice—one of their generals even crucified his own son before a battle to appease the god Baal.

Phoenician crucifixion wasn't very artistic—they normally tied the condemned man to a vertical stake and left him to die of thirst and starvation. The more technically inventive Romans used at least three kinds of crosses: a Y-shaped version, an X-shaped version, and the famous T-shaped model that was used to execute Jesus Christ. Before they were attached to the cross, almost all victims were whipped, beaten, and tortured by having wood slivers, pieces of bone, or other objects (e.g., thorns) driven into their skin. They then had to carry their own crosses to the execution site. To make for a more efficient spectacle, the Romans normally crucified a number of people at the same time.

Common criminals were tied to the cross. Those convicted of more serious crimes were nailed to the frame. Because the bones of the hands are relatively small and weak, nails were driven into each wrist between the two major bones. The feet were nailed to a wooden support block, so that the wrists wouldn't bear the full weight of the body. Christ's death was mercifully brief, at least in comparison to the two or three days it took many condemned men to die. Some unfortunate victims pleaded to be stabbed or more savagely beaten, knowing it would hasten their deaths.

The Romans banned crucifixion about 300 A.D., but it was briefly revived in France in the twelfth century before disappearing once again.

DRAWING AND QUARTERING

In the most ancient form of this horrible method of execution, each of the condemned person's limbs were tied by ropes to four horses, who were then struck by whips so they would gallop away. The limbs were usually severed, then the victim was put out of his misery by beheading.

A much crueler variation developed in England in the seventeenth century. The condemned person was dragged to the site of the execution behind a horse. Then his or her stomach was slit open, and the intestines "drawn out" and tossed into a fire. When it was deemed that the victim had suffered enough, he or she was beheaded, then "quartered" as the limbs were cut off. This brutal practice was finally outlawed by the British Parliament in 1870.

BEHEADING

This swiftest method of death was normally reserved for nobility or others to whom mercy was shown. The Romans and the Greeks considered it the most honorable form of mandatory death. Beheading was introduced to England by William the Conqueror in 1066, and soon became the most popular way to eliminate noble rivals. Henry VIII beheaded no less than three of his wives. As a courtesy to Anne Boleyn, the first of those, he allowed her to send to France for Europe's most skillful bladesman to sever her head.

The French turned beheading into an industry during their Revolution. Dr. Joseph Guillotin was not the inventor of the machine that bears his name; rather, he was instrumental in persuading the French National Assembly to pass a law requiring that machine be used in all executions. The actual inventors of the guillotine were a French surgeon, Dr. Antoine Lewis, and a German harpsichord maker, Tobias Schmidt. Their first test on a human occurred in front of three thousand French citizens on April 25, 1792. It was deemed a success, and was soon in constant action. Curiously, despite his advocacy of the machine, Dr. Guillotin detested the fact that his name was attached to it.

HANGING

This method of execution is both the oldest and most widely practiced of all — even today, it is the most common method of execution outside of the U.S. In earliest times, the victim was tied to a tree branch pulled down to the ground. Then the branch was let go, leaving the victim to slowly strangle. The word "gallows" is derived from the ancient Indo-European root word *"ghalgh,"* meaning "pliant branch."

After the Dark Ages, however, executioners began experimenting to make hanging a "cleaner" or more humane method of execution. The victim was allowed to drop off a platform or fall through a trapdoor. In the best circumstances, the weight of the body snapped the upper spine, producing instant unconsciousness before death.

THE ELECTRIC CHAIR

The lethal nature of electricity was demonstrated when several scientists were accidently killed during experiments in the mid-1800s. In September 1882, the first electric service was provided in New York City. Six years later, the state legislature authorized electrocution as a legal form of execution. However, the new electric companies lobbied vigorously against the law, because they didn't want prospective customers to make the connection between electricity and death.

However, the first electrocution was carried out on August 6, 1890 upon William Kemmler in Auburn. The death took eight minutes and was incredibly gruesome to watch. For the next two decades, a series of similarly botched attempts almost led to the elimination of this form of execution. Today, however, the technique has been refined to the point where unconsciousness comes quickly, and death occurs in a few seconds.

THE GAS CHAMBER

The idea of using gas to execute criminals became popular after the deadly effects of gas were observed on the battlefields of World War I. U.S. Army Major D.A. Turner built the first prototype gas chamber in Nevada. He placed a shallow bowl below a chair, into which cyanide pellets, water, and sulfuric acid could be mixed to create a lethal effect. Turner argued that death would be quick and painless.

However, the first victim, a Chinese immigrant convicted of a gang slaying, took an agonizing six minutes to die. Even today, the average gas chamber death takes eight or nine minutes, and this method of execution is increasingly viewed as unnecessarily cruel.

LETHAL INJECTION

In December 1982, the first execution by lethal injection took place in Texas. Three drugs were introduced by I.V. — a barbiturate to induce unconsciousness, a muscle relaxant to stop the breathing process, and a salt to induce cardiac arrest. Physicians argue that the method is the most humane to date, because the condemned person is unconscious after the first ten to thirty seconds. As more states resume executions, this method is becoming more and more popular.

Who Was "Typhoid Mary"—America's Most Lethal Person?

It is truly unfortunate and cruel that so many people who have been diagnosed "HIV positive" are shunned, as if their virus could be transferred by casual contact.

However, in history there have been specific individuals who carried other diseases that have infected many other people by routine contact. Perhaps none has been so dangerous as "Typhoid Mary Mallon."

Typhus is a disease caused by one of the more than one thousand types of salmonella bacteria carried in human feces and urine. Typhus, which causes high fever and severe diarrhea, has been a powerful killer throughout history: more than twice as many Civil War soldiers died of typhus than were killed on the battlefield. However, a handful of people infected with typhus never experience any symptoms. The bacteria lives within them, to be transmitted to other people if strict sanitary practices aren't followed.

Mary Mallon was one of these typhoid carriers. Three other things made her a killer: by profession, she was a cook; she was none too careful about washing her hands; and she steadfastly refused to admit she carried a dreaded disease. Mary's existence came to light in 1906, when Dr. George Sopher, a New York epidemiologist, began investigating a six-year-long series of typhoid outbreaks. To his astonishment, in case after case, he found that the household or eating establishment had employed an unmarried, stout, middle-aged, Irish, female cook with grey hair, steel-rimmed spectacles, and a sullen disposition. In the year 1900 alone, she had worked for as many as five families, leaving behind several dozen cases of typhus. In 1903, she moved upstate to Ithaca, New York, where she triggered an epidemic of fourteen-hundred cases. Back in the New York area in 1904, four household members of her first employer were hospitalized just two weeks after Mary cooked her first meal.

Sopher finally tracked Typhoid Mary to the kitchen of a Park Avenue penthouse apartment, in which two servants had been hospitalized and the family's daughter had died. When the doctor asked for her cooperation, she came after him with a meat cleaver. Sopher had no choice but to have her forcibly arrested. Stool samples revealed that her gallbladder was teeming with the bacteria. Mary refused to have her gallbladder removed, and she refused to give up her profession. As "public health enemy number one," she was removed to a cottage on an island in New York's City's East River, where she lived and ate alone.

After four years, Mary Mallon relented and promised authorities she would abandon cooking and would work only as a laundress. She was released from confinement — and immediately broke her promise and went back to cooking. For five years, she spawned a long series of typhus outbreaks while staying a step ahead of the furious Dr. Sopher. Finally, in 1915, the epidemiologist went to New York's Sloan Hospital for Women, where twenty-five patients had come down with the debilitating disease. Mary had fled the job just the day before. Hot on her trail, Sopher soon placed her in custody.

This time, her home on North River Island became permanent. She lived in isolation until she died of pneumonia twenty-three years later in 1938. An autopsy revealed that she was still as lethal a carrier as she had been nearly forty years before.

Died with Their Boots On

Fame seems to send a lot of men and women to an early grave. Here's a list of celebrities who died at age forty or younger:

CELEBRITY	AGE
* Ritchie Valens	17
* Sid Vicious	21
* Buddy Holly	22
* Freddie Prinze	22
* Dorothy Stratten	22
* James Dean	24
* Frankie Lymon	25
* Jean Harlow	26
* Brian Jones	26
* Otis Redding	26
* Sharon Tate	26
* Jimi Hendrix	27
* Janis Joplin	27
* Jim Morrison	27
* The Big Bopper	28
* Ronnie Van Zandt	28
* Sam Cooke	29
* Hank Williams	29
* Patsy Cline	30
* Jim Croce	30
* Andy Gibb	30
* Rudolph Valentino	31
* Carole Lombard	32
* Thurman Munson	32

* "Mama" Cass Elliot	33
* Kay Kendall	33
* John Belushi	34
* Bruce Lee	34
* Jayne Mansfield	34
* Andy Kaufman	35
* Inger Stevens	35
* Nick Adams	36
* Rainer Werner Fassbinder	36
* Marilyn Monroe	36
* Lupe Velez	36
* Bobby Darin	37
* Sal Mineo	37
* Robert Walker	37
* Roberto Clemente	38
* Amelia Earhart	38
* John Gilbert	38
* Mario Lanza	38
* Marilyn Miller	38
* Gia Scala	38
* Harry Chapin	39
* Michael Dunn	39
* John Garfield	39
* Carol Haney	39
* Martin Luther King, Jr.	39
* Malcolm X	39
* Jim Reeves	39
* Sabu	39
* Lenny Bruce	40
* John Lennon	40
* Glenn Miller	40
* Jean Seberg	40

What Kills Us?

According to the National Center for Health Statistics, the following are the leading causes of death in the U.S.:

Cause	Percentage of all deaths
1. Heart disease	38.2%
2. Cancer	21.9%
3. Stroke	7.7%
4. Accidents	4.6%
5. Pulmonary disease	3.3%
6. Pneumonia and influenza	2.8%
7. Diabetes	1.8%
8. Suicide	1.4%
9. Homicide	1.3%
10. Liver disease	1.3%

What are your odds of dying in the next twelve months?

Your Age	White Male	White Female	Black Male	Black Female
25	561 to 1	1754 to 1	311 to 1	943 to 1
35	552 to 1	1136 to 1	200 to 1	483 to 1
45	242 to 1	438 to 1	101 to 1	209 to 1
55	89 to 1	172 to 1	48 to 1	91 to 1
65	37 to 1	73 to 1	25 to 1	46 to 1
75	16 to 1	30 to 1	151 to 1	24 to 1

Another way to look at life expectancy is to examine what percentage of all babies born live to a certain age:

Age	% men surviving	% women surviving
1	98.7%	98.9%
20	97.5%	98.3%
30	95.8%	97.7%
40	93.9%	96.8%
50	89.8%	94.5%
60	80.1%	88.9%
65	72.0%	84.1%
70	61.1%	77.3%
75	47.9%	67.9%
80	33.4%	55.3%
85	19.5%	39.3%

Five

The Facts of Life

What Are Your Chances of Celebrating Your 100th Birthday?

A 1992 survey of one thousand adults by the Alliance for Aging Research revealed that sixty-six percent wanted to live to be one hundred. Would-be centurians included seventy percent of men vs. sixty-two percent of women. Both men and women had a lot of confidence in their longevity, with sixty-nine percent believing they'd live longer than the current average life expectancy of seventy-five years.

What are their chances of achieving their goal? The younger they are, the better. The U.S. Census Bureau found that the number of Americans who had actually reached the century mark increased from 14,710 in 1980 to an estimated thirty-five thousand in 1990. That number will soar to one-hundred thousand by the year 2000. Of all current centurians, about one in eleven were age 105 or older. Although more men want to live to be one hundred, three-quarters of those who've reached that milestone are women.

Today's centurians survived odds of four hundred to one to reach their ripe old age. However, the Census Bureau estimates that the odds of a person born in 1980 reaching age 100 are just eighty-seven to one. Odds of reaching age 105 are 559 to one, while the chances of celebrating a 110th birthday are a very slim 4,762 to one.

And what about your odds of achieving the more modest goal of exceeding the average life expectancy? Currently, forty-eight percent of men and sixty-eight percent of women live to celebrate their seventy-sixth birthday. And Americans age eighty-five and older are currently the fastest growing of all age groups. The 3.3 million people age eighty-five and over are expected to increase to 4.9 million by the year 2000 and thirteen million by 2040.

What Is Leap Year?

1992 was a "leap year," which meant it had 366 days. The extra day, as we all know, is tacked onto February, the shortest month. Where did this calendar curiosity come from, and why do we use it?

Our 365-day calendar dates all the way back to Julius Caesar, who realized that it actually takes 365 days, five hours, and 48½ minutes for the Earth to make one revolution around the sun. In order to prevent the calendar from becoming so screwy that the Ides of March would eventually occur in the fall, the Romans added an extra day every four years.

However, the Roman calendar added an extra forty-six minutes every four years, which meant that the calendar was one day off every 130 years. So in 1582, Pope Gregory XIII decreed that ten days be omitted from that year. In addition, he ordained that there would be no leap year in century years divisible by one hundred—only century years divisible by four hundred. That means that the year 2000 will be a leap year, even though 1700, 1800, and 1900 weren't. This system, clumsy as it seems, will keep our calendar accurate all the way until the year 5388, when people will have to find a way to add an extra day.

That extra day during a leap year is a plus for some, a minus for others. If you're paid by the hour, you gain an extra day's pay; if you're paid by the month, you work an extra day for free. The government collects about $2 billion in extra taxes during leap year; landlords provide services an extra day for free. And all of us get a day older.

The oldest tradition connected with the extra day is that women are allowed to propose to men during any leap year. The origin: a Scottish law passed in 1288, which read, "For il yeare knowne as lepe year, ilk mayden ladye of bothe highe and lowe estat shall Law liberte to bespeke ye man she likes."

America, The Melting Pot

In the last half of the 1980s, nearly five million immigrants took up legal permanent residence in the U.S., a group so large that they made up one in four of the foreign-born residents of the U.S. The 1990 Census found that 19.8 million Americans were born in other countries, 7.9% of the population. While almost double the 1970 figure (4.7%), it's nowhere near the fifteen percent of our population that were foreign-born in 1900.

Leading countries of origin of the new immigrants were Mexico (ten percent), the Philippines (eight percent), and Korea (six percent). Of all foreign-born Americans, over four times as many come from Mexico (21.7%) as the number two country (Philippines, 4.8%). Also in the top five are Canada, Cuba, and Germany.

Foreign-born residents make up 70.4% of the population of Hialeah, Florida, 59.7% of the population of Miami, Florida, 59.4% of the population of Huntington Park, California, and 55.1% of the population of Union City, New Jersey. More than one in five Californians were born in another country, followed by New York (15.9%), Hawaii (14.7%), Florida (12.9%), and New Jersey (12.5%) What about illegal aliens? Although accurate figures are impossible to come by, some experts estimate there may be as many as twenty million in the U.S. The U.S. Immigration Service captures and deports almost 1.5 million illegal aliens per year, but estimates that another three to four million enter the country but escape detection. A whopping ninety-seven percent of captured illegal aliens are from Mexico.

Why Do Our Ears Pop in an Elevator or an Airplane?

Air pressure drops about .1 inch of mercury for every one hundred feet in elevation. When our elevation increases rapidly, in an airplane taking off or in an elevator, the outside pressure drops more quickly than our inside pressure, producing discomfort in our ears. The "pop" we feel is air escaping through our Eustachian tubes to even the pressure. If our Eustachian tube is blocked, perhaps as a result of a cold, the pressure of air pushing outward against the eardrum can produce excruciating pain. The best way to relieve the pressure is to yawn, chew gum, or hold your nose and blow with your mouth closed.

When we descend, the situation is reversed. The outside air pressure rises more quickly and pushes inward against our eardrums, causing pain until the pressure equalizes.

Do Rainmakers Really Make Rain?

Since before the dawn of recorded time, people in drought-stricken areas have been praying, dancing, or performing a wide variety of rituals to produce precipitation—and they still are. In 1992, tens of thousands of people rioted in Somalia because they believed that country's severe drought was caused by women wearing short skirts. (Hmmm, maybe that's why it doesn't rain often in Los Angeles.)

Anyway, the ultimate effectiveness of prayer and rain dancing is hard to determine scientifically. But a lot of supposedly "scientific" methods developed by self-proclaimed "rainmakers" have been downright frauds. One such wizard, Charles Hatfield, was immortalized in the famous 1956 Burt Lancaster movie, *The Rainmaker.* Hatfield proclaimed that he could attract rain clouds by boiling a mixture of secret chemicals on top of tall towers. After a number of widely publicized successes (and some very quiet failures), the city of San Diego agreed to pay him $10,000 to fill nearly empty city reservoirs. Within hours after brewing up his stew, torrential rains began to fall. Streets were flooded, houses washed away, and a dam broke.

As a result, Hatfield was hit with a barrage of lawsuits. The California Supreme Court finally settled the issue by dismissing the suits on the grounds that rain is an act of God. Hatfield was thrilled—until the San Diego city council proclaimed that since rain was an act of God, the city didn't have to pay the rainmaker his $10,000.

Many other entrepreneurs have concocted rainmaking schemes from firing rockets into clouds to aiming invisible beams. The results have been uniformly unreliable. Methods of creating rain clouds are doomed to failure because of the immense volume of water vapor they must contain. A government study showed that one small thunderstorm cloud held more than thirty-three million gallons of water.

A more practical approach is encouraging the formation of ice crystals in clouds that already exist. That goal was first accomplished in 1947, when three pounds of crushed dry ice were scattered over a cloud. The carbon dioxide crystals attracted supercooled water, forming snowflakes that melted and fell as rain. This technique, which provides the "seed" for the formation of precipitation, is called "cloud seeding."

Shortly afterwards, cloud seeders began using silver iodide, a compound with an atomic structure very similar to ice crystals. Cloud seeding has proven to be of some usefulness in increasing the amount of precipitation that falls from existing clouds. But it is of no use in the dry air over drought-stricken areas.

What Causes Wind?

Wind is created by differences in air pressure between two air masses. Differences in air pressure are caused by uneven heating of the Earth's surface. As air warms, the molecules expand and rise, reducing the air pressure. Cold, dense air flows in to replace it, creating wind.

To picture how air molecules move from high pressure to low pressure, picture a seesaw with round Ping-Pong balls (representing air molecules) on each end. If the air pressure is the same, there's no movement and no wind. If the air pressure is lower on one end, the air molecules on the higher end roll "downhill" toward it, creating movement. The greater the pressure difference (the steeper the slope), the faster the air molecules (wind) move.

To compute how fast a ball would roll down a hill,

you would have to use formulas based on the weight of the ball and the angle of the slope. To forecast how strong winds will be, meteorologists have formulas that use exact differences in air pressure (the weight of the air) and the distances between air masses (the height of the slope) to compute a statistic called the "pressure gradient force."

Slight differences in pressure produce a lower pressure gradient force, resulting in only gentle breezes. A good example is the breeze that develops near a large body of water. During the day, the land warms more quickly than the water, so the cooler air moves toward the land to create an onshore breeze. At night, the land cools more quickly, so the breeze turns around and blows off shore toward the warmer water.

When a large low-pressure system collides with a high-pressure system, the result is often gale force winds. The most destructive winds, those of hurricanes and tornadoes, result when air rushes toward the extremely low pressure at the eye of the storm.

What Is Lightning?

For some reason scientists still don't completely understand, friction resulting from the interaction of wind, water droplets, and ice particles causes separation of positive and negative electrical charges inside a thundercloud and on the ground. Lightning results when electricity travels between areas of opposite electrical charges within a cloud, between two clouds, or, about twenty percent of the time, between a cloud and the ground. Lightning detection systems have recorded an average of forty million cloud-to-ground strikes each year, an average of thirteen for every square mile in the United States each year.

You should be glad you don't have to pay the electric bill for lightning, because the current in just one bolt is so enormous a storm could bankrupt even Ross Perot. Measurements have been recorded of bolts containing up to 345,000 amperes, enough electricity to service two hundred-thousand homes. Pressure of the electricity in lightning can exceed fifteen million volts. A single thunderstorm can produce continuous releases of energy greater than a million kilowatts.

The discharge of lightning begins when a mass of negative electrons builds up so much energy that it overcomes air's normally high resistance to electric current. A channel of electrons a few inches in diameter (a "leader") forces its way downward in a series of steps about 150 feet long. This motion is the reason lightning looks jagged instead of straight.

When the "leader" nears the ground, it draws a "streamer" positive electrons toward it, normally through something high such as a tree or a lightning rod. When the two meet, they form a pencil-thin path for an electric current to flow from ground to cloud.

A microsecond after this path is formed, an intensely brilliant flash we call lightning surges FROM GROUND TO CLOUD along the path created by the streamer. This flash, called the "return stroke," is the light we actually see. The wave of positive electrons traveling upwards moves at sixty thousand miles per second, about one-third the speed of light. Several waves of electricity can make the round-trip in less than one second, which is why lightning often seems to flicker.

Can lightning strike twice in the same place? It not only can, it often does. For example, the top of the Empire State Building has been struck a dozen times in a single storm and as often as five hundred times in a year.

What Is Deodorant and Why Do We Need It?

In comedy skits and cartoons, spraying Raid under the armpits satirizes terrible personal hygiene. That's why you'll probably be surprised to learn that you probably do the same thing every morning.

The reason? Perspiration is totally odorless. However, perspiration that comes from pores on the scalp, in the groin, and in the armpits contains about one percent fat. Bacteria on the skin go to work on these fats, eventually producing unpleasant odors in the same way that decaying food starts to smell. Deodorants aren't just good-smelling stuff, but rather contain insecticides and bactericides to stop the unpleasant varmints before they complete their work. NOTE: Don't switch to Raid—it's far too harsh for human skin.

Does Skin Really Shrivel under Water?

After lounging around in the bath for a half an hour or so, the skin on our hands and feet looks like it's shrinking from the cleanliness. But the opposite is true—the wrinkles are actually produced when the skin expands.

Here's how it works. Our bodily fluids are more concentrated than fresh water, so our skin gradually absorbs water when it's submerged for awhile. The skin over most of our body is so thin that we don't notice the absorption. However, the skin on our palms, fingers, soles of our feet, and toes is very thick. When these areas absorb water, it expands and forms wrinkles. That skin looks whiter than usual because the extra fluid makes it more opaque.

However, you could bathe in the ocean for hours with nary a wrinkle. The reason: The concentration of salt water just about matches the concentration of our bodily fluids, so little or none is absorbed.

The Real Facts about Firearms

Most Americans know the grim fact that 46,752 U.S. soldiers were killed in battle in Viet Nam between 1963 and 1973. But hardly anyone knows that nearly twice as many Americans—84,633—were killed by firearms right in our own country during the same period. As a matter of fact, since 1900, there have been more Americans killed by handguns in the U.S. than have been killed in all of our foreign wars combined, including World War I and World War II.

There are more than 150 million privately owned firearms in the U.S., with about half of all households containing at least one. Even though a significant number of gun owners list self-protection as a major reason for owning a weapon, studies show that guns are far more likely to injure innocent parties. For every criminal shot dead in self-protection, there were forty-three accidental deaths, homicides, or suicides. Members of a household owning a weapon were eighteen times more likely to be shot than a criminal, and friends of the household were twelve times more likely to be shot.

Firearms are the weapon of choice in sixty percent of all murders. About one in five victims is cut and stabbed, while about fifteen percent of victims are beaten or battered to death.

America's Mental Health

When we watch the news, it seems that almost everyone is crazy. Still, it's sobering to realize how widespread real mental illness is in our society. A massive study by the National Institutes of Health showed that as many as thirty-eight percent of all Americans have or once had a recognized psychiatric disorder. About twenty percent of those surveyed reported a mental problem within six months of the survey date.

Who suffers from serious mental problems during their lifetimes?:

* Thirteen percent of Americans will suffer from alcohol abuse.
* Eleven percent will experience some phobia, such as fear of heights.
* Six percent will experience a major depression.
* Six percent will become dependent on drugs.

* Three percent will suffer from an antisocial or obsessive-compulsive disorder.
* Two percent will suffer from a panic disorder or mental impairment.
* .2% (one in five hundred) will suffer from schizophrenia, severe sleep problems, or anorexia nervosa.

Why Are There Twenty-four Hours in a Day and Sixty Minutes in an Hour?

Most of us know that a "day" is the time it takes the Earth to revolve once on its axis, and a year is the time it takes for the Earth to make one complete revolution around the sun. But you may be surprised to learn that there are absolutely no logical reasons why a week consists of seven days, why a day is divided into twenty-four hours, and why an hour is divided into sixty minutes.

The Babylonians were the first to use a seven-day week. The reason: They recognized seven heavenly bodies (the sun, the moon, Mercury, Venus, Mars, Jupiter, and Saturn), so they worshiped one each day. However, the Romans used an eight-day week, and other civilizations used periods of time ranging from four to ten days. The biblical story of creation eventually settled the issue; God created the Earth in six days and rested on the seventh. As Christianity spread, the seven-day week became standard.

Those frisky Babylonians also originated the sixty-second minute and sixty-minute hour. The reason: They considered sixty a mystical number, because it could be divided by so many other numbers (one, two, three, four, five, six, ten, twelve, fifteen, twenty, and thirty). Logically, it would seem a system based on tens would have been easier—in fact, for thirteen years following its Revolution, France established a day with ten hours consisting of one hundred minutes of one hundred seconds. But when Napoleon took over, the old method was reestablished.

And why do we have a twenty-four-hour day? This time the Egyptians are the source. They divided the night into twelve different segments marked by the rising of twelve different constellations. The day was divided into ten segments, plus separate segments for dawn and dusk. The total: twenty-four segments or "hours." So, if you don't find enough hours in the day to get everything done, blame the pharaohs.

Sex: Who's Doing What with Whom?

Is America a nation of swingers? Not according to the latest (1990-1991) surveys of American sexual practices conducted by the National Center for Health Statistics and the National Opinion Research Center of the University of Chicago. In fact, both these highly reputable organizations report that Americans are now down-right Puritans.

NUMBER OF SEXUAL PARTNERS
An astounding seventy percent of Americans age

eighteen to sixty-five reported that they'd had just one sex partner in the last twelve months, while another eighteen percent had no sex partners at all. That means nearly nine in ten Americans were either monogamous or chaste over a year. Only six percent reported two partners, two percent reported three partners, and four percent reported four partners or more. One of the most striking findings was that twenty-two percent of men ages eighteen to twenty-nine reported no sex partners in a year, compared with 9.7% in a study conducted a decade earlier. The other revealing finding: Casual sex is rare, with only six percent of men and one percent of women responding that they'd had sex with someone they "picked up."

Over a lifetime, the average American will have had seven partners. The average is lowest for people who have long-term marriages (five partners) and highest for men and women who've been divorced (thirteen partners).

FREQUENCY OF SEX

The average American adult had sex fifty-seven times per year. The figure was highest for couples that described themselves as "happy" (seventy-five times per year) and lowest for those who described their marriages as "not too happy" (forty-three times per year). Married couples under age thirty had sex an average of 105 times, the highest for any age group.

MARITAL FIDELITY

About twenty percent of men and ten percent of women reported having sex partners other than their spouses. Prime age range for infidelity was thirty to forty-four.

PREMARITAL SEX
Seventy-five percent of women said that they had had sex before they were married, and sixty-eight percent of never-married women had been sexually active. About two-thirds of teenagers had had sex by age eighteen and eighty percent by age nineteen.

CONTRACEPTION
About sixteen percent of women were at risk of unwanted pregnancy because they seldom or ever used any form of contraception. The most popular form of contraception for married couples was sterilization, with the rate soaring from eighteen percent to thirty-six percent of all couples in the last decade. Use of birth control pills plummeted among married couples but were still the most popular form of birth control among single women (twenty-five percent).

HOMOSEXUALITY
Four recent studies, including the two mentioned previously, indicated that between 1.5% and four percent of American adults considered themselves homosexual or bisexual. These results are far below the ten percent level in the famous Kinsey Report done in 1950. Eighty percent of Americans said that they "strongly disapproved" of homosexuality.

Now, That's a Crime

Among the many experiences Americans have in common is that almost all of us, at one time or another, are a victim of crime. How often do crimes take place? The following list may surprise you:

Crime	How frequently it occurs
Larceny-theft	Every 4 seconds
Burglary	Every 10 seconds
Motor vehicle theft	Every 20 seconds
Aggravated assault	Every 33 seconds
Robbery	Every 55 seconds
Forcible rape	Every 6 minutes
Murder	Every 24 minutes

What are the most popular pastimes for law-breakers? According to the F.B.I., they are, in order:

1. Larceny/theft
2. Driving under the influence
3. Drug abuse violations
4. Assault
5. Drunkenness
6. Disorderly conduct
7. Burglary
8. Aggravated assault
9. Fraud
10. Vandalism

And how much do the bad guys get? Following is the "take" from the average crime:

1.	Bank robbery	$3,013
2.	General residential burglary	$1,107
3.	Nighttime residential burglary	$1,085
4.	Robbery of commercial property	$1,017
5.	Office burglary	$ 914
6.	Robbery in residence	$ 796
7.	Miscellaneous robbery	$ 668
8.	Theft from buildings	$ 665
9.	Misc. larceny-theft	$ 591
10.	Theft from motor vehicle	$ 434

What kind of crimes lead to the longest sentences? Vicious crimes against people:

Crime	Average sentence in months
1. Forcible rape, victim dies	416.5
2. Armed robbery, victim shot dead	365.2
3. Other murder	349.5
4. Forcible rape, with forced oral sex	202.1
5. Vehicular homicide while driving drunk	141.2
6. Selling cocaine for resale	126.3

7. Armed robbery where victim is shot but recovers 123.4
8. Arson with damages more than $500,000 .... 99.9
9. Assault with gun, knife, or pipe, victim recovers 92.7
10. Armed robbery, victim not hurt 68.0

Everything You Want to Know about Christmas

Despite the gloomy economic news of the last few years, we Americans apparently haven't stopped celebrating Christmas in a big way, as the following facts show:

CHRISTMAS GIFTS

In 1991, Americans spent $80 billion on Christmas presents, which works out to $375 per household. You used an astounding 320,000 miles of wrapping paper costing $500 million to wrap an average of thirty gifts per family. The U.S. Post Office transported 2.3 billion Christmas cards.

CHRISTMAS EATING

We celebrated the holidays with $1 billion in liquor and $2 billion in food. That includes eighty-nine million hams, sixty-eight million turkeys, twenty million pounds of fruitcake, one hundred-twenty million pounds of eggnog, twenty million bottles of champagne, and 1.7 billion cookies. Since Christmas means sharing, eighty-four million of those cookies were left out for Santa Claus. Almost ten percent of those cookies were left out in households with no children—we wonder exactly who was expected to eat these.

CHRISTMAS TREES

Traditionalists will be happy to discover that real trees still outnumber artificial trees, albeit by a paper-thin margin. Americans purchased 36.5 million real trees, enough to forest every square foot of Rhode Island. 36.2 million households displayed artificial trees. The average tree is illuminated by 350 lights, with half of all households preferring multicolored lights and half all-white lights. Cost of operating these lights for a month runs about $2.10. Americans also used 160,000 miles of garlands and 3.6 million miles of tinsel.

CHRISTMAS SERVICES

About 210,000,000 Americans are Christians, but only thirty-nine percent of them managed to make it to religious services last Christmas. Bad weather isn't an excuse—only one out of four people could look outside and see snow last Christmas.

What's A Trillion Dollars?

In 1992, the national debt exceeded $3.5 trillion, or $3,500,000,000,000. If you have trouble imagining what a trillion dollars really is, you may be interested to know that $1 trillion would buy:

* A forty-hour-week paycheck at the minimum wage for every person in the world.
* A 1991-1992 Harvard tuition for every person under age eighteen in the U.S.
* Two weeks at Club Med in Bora Bora, French Polynesia, for all Americans age eighteen or older.
* An in-ground concrete swimming pool for every house in the U.S.
* One large pepperoni pizza and a soft drink per day for a year for every person in the U.S.

What Is Humidity and What Does It Mean to Us?

"Humidity" is the amount of water vapor in the air, a measurement that doesn't tell us much about how comfortable we are or what the weather is likely to be. For example, the air during a heavy winter snowstorm in the U.S. contains less moisture than the cloudless skies over the Sahara Desert. The amount of water vapor in 60°F air in San Francisco would bring a damp, bone-chilling fog and drizzle, but would contribute to a comfortable, brilliantly sunny beach day in 85°F sunny Los Angeles.

The reason is the likelihood of precipitation and the degree to which the air feels damp or dry doesn't depend on the amount of water vapor in a specific volume, but rather the actual amount of water relative to the maximum amount of water the air could hold at that temperature. This ratio is called the "relative humidity"; when your local weatherperson says the "humidity" is sixty-five percent, he or she really means the "relative humidity" is sixty-five percent — in other words, the air holds about two-thirds of the water vapor it could potentially hold. The relative humidity constantly changes with the temperature.

We see the importance of relative humidity every winter in the northern United States. Freezing air holds very little moisture. When that air enters our homes and is heated to 70°F, the relative humidity plunges to levels lower than the driest deserts. To return the humidity to comfortable levels, we purchase humidifiers to put water vapor into the air. In the summer, on the other hand, warm air descends to our basements, which tend to be cooler than the rest of the house. The result is dampness that can produce mildew, unless we run a dehumidifier to take water out of the air.

Relative humidity has other practical applications. For example, clothes can hang on a line all day without drying when the humidity is eighty-five percent or ninety percent. On the other hand, dehydration during exercise is a danger when the humidity is very low — perspiration evaporates so quickly that we feel cool until we run out of fluid and overheat.

Relative humidity also helps us understand our external weather, too. For example, you can see why we get our heaviest rains when cold air runs into warm, damp air. On the other hand, the weather clears when warm air replaces cold, damp air. When the relative humidity is close to one hundred percent during the day, we're likely to have fog at night when the air cools.

How They Make That Fur Coat

Next to abortion, the subject of fur coats may be the most explosive ethical question in the U.S. No matter what side you're on, you might be interested in how many animals of various species have to be killed to make just one coat:

Animal	Pelts per coat
Mink	60
Sable	50
Muskrat	50
Opossum	45
Red fox	42
Raccoon	40
Otter	20
Lynx	18
Coyote	16
Beaver	15

How Do You Spend Your Money?

We all ask, "Where does our money go?" Well, the U.S. Bureau of Labor Statistics conducts surveys to find out. You will probably be astounded to learn that the top expense of the average household, consuming almost one-quarter of all money spent, is not shelter, but automobile expense. That's right, the cost of gasoline, installment payments, insurance, repairs, tolls, etc., eats up 24.7% of the average American's expenditures. The list:

Expense	Percentage of expenditures
Vehicle expense	24.7%
Shelter	20.2%
Food and alcohol	19.4%
Utilities	8.2%
Entertainment	5.8%
Apparel and services	5.2%
Miscellaneous	7.1%
Health care	4.0%
Household furnishings	3.9%
Household operations	1.4%

The Electronic Home

As we plunge head-on into the information age, our homes are filling up with an increasing variety of electronic toys. As of 1992, here's what our homes contained:

Equipment	% of U.S. homes
Radio	98%
Television	98%
Color television	97%
Audio system	94%

Videocassette recorder	77%
Two or more television sets	64%
Basic cable	59%
Preprogrammed videocassettes	52%
Telephone answering device	46%
Cordless telephone	41%
Compact disc player	35%
Home computer	33%
Color television with stereo	31%
One or more pay cable channels	28%
Camcorder	17%
Home security system	16%
Projection television	8%
LCD television	6%
Satellite dish	3%
Cellular telephone	3%
Home fax device	1%
Laser disc player	1%

Diamonds Are a Girl's Best Friend

Diamonds have been among mankind's most prized possessions since the dawn of time. Diamonds, made entirely of crystalized carbon, are most valuable when absolutely colorless. However, they are found in a variety of colors, from jet black to blue to green to, rarely, red. The largest diamond ever found was a 3,106-carat stone (a carat is .2 of a gram, so this stone was 651 grams or about twenty-one ounces) found in South Africa in 1905. From this huge stone was cut the "Star of Africa," the world's largest cut diamond at 530.2 carats.

The Star of Africa is now part of the British Royal Sceptre.

The highest price ever paid for a diamond was the $12,760,000 bid for a 101.84-carat stone auctioned in Switzerland in 1990. The highest price per carat was $926,315 for a nearly one-carat stone auctioned in New York in 1987.

Six

The Best and Worst

The Best and Worst Foods

If you talk to an eight-year-old, you'll learn that ice cream and candy bars are the best food, while spinach and broccoli are the worst. On the more serious side, some nutritionists evaluated all foods, giving positive value to complex carbohydrates, protein, fiber, vitamins, etc., and negative value to saturated fats, sugars, etc. They ended up with the list of the ten best and ten worst foods:

Ten Best Foods
   1. Turnip greens

2. Raw chopped spinach
3. Bok choy
4. Whole Wheat Total Cereal
5. Cooked mustard greens
6. Total Corn Flakes Cereal
7. Cooked beet greens
8. Product 19 Cereal
9. Fresh parsley
10. Raw broccoli

Ten Worst (Least Healthy) Foods
1. Sweetbreads
2. Scrambled eggs
3. Caviar
4. Little Debbie Snack Cakes
5. Gatorade
6. Lipton Iced Tea
7. Salted butter
8. Coconut oil
9. Heavy cream
10. Soft drinks with caffeine

Longest Runs at the Top of the *Billboard* Album Charts

Think Elvis or the Beatles holds the record for the album with the longest consecutive period of time atop the *Billboard* magazine charts? The Beatles don't even make the list. Instead, the all-time longevity champ is Leonard Bernstein's score to a Broadway musical. Here's the list:

1. *West Side Story* soundtrack (1962)   54 weeks
2. *Thriller* Michael Jackson (1983)   37 weeks
3. *South Pacific* soundtrack (1958)   31 weeks
4. *Calypso* Harry Belafonte (1956)   31 weeks
5. *Rumours* Fleetwood Mac (1977)   31 weeks
6. *Saturday Night Fever* soundtrack (1978)   24 weeks
7. *Purple Rain* Prince (1984)   24 weeks
8. *Blue Hawaii* Elvis Presley (1961)   20 weeks
9. *More of the Monkees* the Monkees (1967)   18 weeks
10. *Dirty Dancing* soundtrack (1988)   18 weeks

Best of International Business

We truly live in a global economy, and major U.S. corporations must now slug it out with their foreign competitors all over the world to survive. One measure of how companies are doing is how widely their names are known around the world. Six of the ten most familiar brands are American:

1. Coca-Cola
2. McDonald's
3. Pepsi-Cola
4. Sony
5. Kodak
6. Toyota
7. Nestlé
8. Disney
9. Honda
10. Ford

***

In terms of most respected brands, we're not doing as well. The top ten:

1. Sony
2. Mercedes-Benz
3. Rolls-Royce
4. IBM
5. Disney
6. Coca-Cola
7. Duracell
8. Levi's
9. Kodak
10. Panasonic

When familiarity and respect are combined, the following are the "most powerful" global brand names:

1. Coca-Cola
2. Sony
3. Mercedes-Benz
4. Kodak
5. Disney
6. Nestlé
7. Toyota
8. McDonald's
9. IBM
10. Pepsi-Cola

America's Busiest Roads

Want to get stuck in a monster traffic jam? The most crowded stretch of road on the entire interstate highway system is the George Washington Bridge on I-95, which connects New Jersey with Manhattan—a span traversed by almost a quarter of a million cars per day. Following is a list of the ten worst stretches of highway:

Highway	Average daily vehicles
1. I-95, George Washington Bridge, New York City	249,300
2. I-90/94, Dan Ryan/ Kennedy Expressway, Chicago	248,000
3. I-10, Santa Monica/San Bernardino Freeway, Los Angeles	243,000
4. I-5, Seattle	224,000
5. Oakland Bay Bridge, San Francisco	223,000
6. I-35, Dallas	217,700
7. I-10, New Orleans	187,600
8. I-610, Houston	169,000
9. 1-95, Miami	169,000
10. I-5, San Diego	161,000

The Best and Worst Jobs

The *Jobs Rated Almanac* evaluated ninety different factors (from stress to income to job security) of 250 careers to arrive at the following rankings of the best and worst jobs:

The Best Jobs
 1. Actuary
 2. Computer programmer
 3. Computer systems analyst
 4. Mathematician
 5. Statistician
 6. Hospital administrator
 7. Industrial engineer
 8. Physicist
 9. Astrologer
10. Paralegal

The Worst Jobs
 1. Migrant farm worker
 2. Fisherman
 3. Construction worker
 4. Roofer
 5. Seaman
 6. Dairy farmer
 7. Roustabout
 8. Lumberjack
 9. Cowboy
10. NFL football player

What about money? The best paying careers are:

1. Surgeon
2. Psychiatrist
3. Doctor of Osteopathy
4. Chiropractor
5. Dentist/Orthodontist
6. Veterinarian
7. Aerospace/civil engineer
8. Attorney
9. Industrial/mechanical/electrical engineer
10. Psychologist

And the worst paying jobs?

1. Private child care worker
2. Food counter worker
3. Nonprivate child care worker
4. Cleaners and servants
5. Kitchen workers
6. Food preparation workers
7. Waiter's assistants
8. Cashiers
9. Waiters and waitresses
10. Textile sewing machine operators

Who Gets the Best Damage Awards from Juries?

We all hope that tragedy doesn't befall us or our families. On the other hand, if we're the victims of negligence, we want the guilty parties to pay. Following is, in order, the tragedies that elicit the highest damages:

1. Death
2. Brain damage
3. Amputation
4. Paraplegia
5. Quadraplegia
6. Emotional distress
7. Leg injuries
8. Multiple injuries
9. Burns
10. Disk injury

The Best American Novels

For his book *The Best and Worst of Everything*, Les Krantz pored through bibliographic references and evaluated other criteria to rank, in order, the ten greatest American novels:

1. *The Adventures of Huckleberry Finn* by Mark Twain
2. *Moby Dick* by Herman Melville
3. *Gravity's Rainbow* by Thomas Pynchon
4. *The Scarlet Letter* by Nathaniel Hawthorne
5. *Absalom, Absalom!* by William Faulkner
6. *The Great Gatsby* by F. Scott Fitzgerald
7. *The Sound and the Fury* by William Faulkner
8. *The Portrait of a Lady* by Henry James
9. *As I Lay Dying* by William Faulkner
10. *Light in August* by William Faulkner

The Most Anthologized English Poems

The value of a poem, like beauty, is in the eye of the beholder. But one measure of a poem's importance is its inclusion in poetry anthology. According to the *Concise Columbia Book of Poetry,* the following are the ten most anthologized English poems:

1. "The Tyger" by William Blake
2. "Sir Patrick Spens" Anonymous [often spelled as "Sir Patrick Spence"]
3. "To Autumn" by John Keats
4. "That Time of Year Thou Mayst in Me Behold" by William Shakespeare
5. "Pied Beauty" by Gerard Manley Hopkins
6. "Stopping by the Woods on a Snowy Evening" by Robert Frost
7. "Kubla Khan" by Samuel Taylor Coleridge
8. "Dover Beach" by Matthew Arnold
9. *"La Belle Dame sans Merci"* by John Keats
10. "To the Virgins, to Make Much of Time" by Robert Herrick

America's Most Scenic Highways

According to the *Rand McNally Road Atlas,* the following are America's most scenic highways:

1. Pacific Coast Highway, California
2. Columbia Gorge Highway, Oregon

3. Coastal Highway, Maine
4. Going-to-the-Sun Road, Glacier National Park, Montana
5. Skyline Drive/Blue Ridge Highway, Virginia
6. Million-dollar Highway, Colorado
7. Oak Creek Canyon Drive, Arizona
8. Highway 7, Arkansas

Most Popular TV Series

According to the ratings people, A.C. Nielsen, the following were the most popular shows in every decade from the 1950s through 1992:

The 1950s
1. "Arthur Godfrey's Talent Scouts"
2. "I Love Lucy"
3. "You Bet Your Life"
4. "Dragnet"
5. "The Jack Benny Show"
6. "Arthur Godfrey and Friends"
7. "Gunsmoke"
8. "The Red Skelton Show"
9. "December Bride"
10. "I've Got a Secret"

The 1960s
1. "Bonanza"
2. "The Red Skelton Show"
3. "The Andy Griffith Show"
4. "The Beverly Hillbillies"
5. "The Ed Sullivan Show"

6. "The Lucy Show"/"Here's Lucy"
7. "The Jackie Gleason Show"
8. "Bewitched"
9. "Gomer Pyle"
10. "Candid Camera"

The 1970s

1. "All in the Family"
2. "M*A*S*H*"
3. "Hawaii Five-O"
4. "Happy Days"
5. "The Waltons"
6. "The Mary Tyler Moore Show"
7. "Sanford and Son"
8. "One Day at a Time"
9. "Three's Company"
10. "60 Minutes"

The 1980s

1. "60 Minutes"
2. "Dallas"
3. "The Cosby Show"
4. "Dynasty"
5. "Knots Landing"
6. "Cheers"
7. "Magnum, P.I."
8. "Murder, She Wrote"
9. "Who's the Boss?"
10. "Family Ties"

1990-1992

1. "60 Minutes"
2. "Cheers"

3. "Roseanne"
4. "Murphy Brown"
5. "Designing Women"
6. "Monday Night Football"
7. "Murder, She Wrote"
8. "A Different World"
9. "Unsolved Mysteries"
10. "Full House"

The Most Popular Movies

Because of inflation, it's impossible to rank the biggest box-office attractions of the last fifty or sixty years. The fairest way is to give you lists of the most popular films by decade since before 1930:

Pre-1930
1. *The Birth of a Nation*
2. *The Big Parade*
3. *The Singing Fool*

1930-39
1. *Gone With the Wind*
2. *Snow White and the Seven Dwarfs*
3. *King Kong*
4. *The Wizard of Oz*
5. *San Francisco*

1940-49
1. *Cinderella*
2. *Pinocchio*
3. *Song of the South*

4. *Fantasia*
5. *Bambi*

1950-59
1. *Lady and the Tramp*
2. *Ben Hur*
3. *Around the World in 80 Days*
4. *Sleeping Beauty*

1960-69
1. *The Sound of Music*
2. *Doctor Zhivago*
3. *Butch Cassidy and the Sundance Kid*
4. *Mary Poppins*
5. *The Graduate*

1970-79
1. *Star Wars*
2. *Jaws*
3. *Grease*
4. *The Exorcist*
5. *The Godfather*

1980-89
1. *E.T. — The Extra-Terrestrial*
2. *Return of the Jedi*
3. *Batman*
4. *The Empire Strikes Back*
5. *Ghostbusters*

Seven

Fun Food Facts

History of the Hamburger

Cooking was difficult for nomadic tribesmen always on the move through rugged terrain. On the other hand, raw meat was very difficult to chew. One solution was developed by a tribe of Turkish-speaking people who roamed Central Asia. These people, known as the Tartars, placed a piece of goat, camel, or horse meat underneath their saddles at the beginning of the day. By nightfall, the action of the saddle had pounded it to bits. The Tartars would scrape up the minced meat, season it, and eat it raw. It's hard to find goat, camel, or horse meat today, but when raw ground beef is served, it's called Steak Tartar.

In the nineteenth century, a merchant from the town of Hamburg, Germany, tasted the ground beef during a trip to Asia, then introduced the concept back home, calling it "Hamburg steak." At some point, people who found raw ground beef unpalatable decided to cook it. The cooked version was called "hamburger meat."

German immigrants brought the recipe to the United States. The dish became widely popular after patties on buns were served at the famous St. Louis World's Fair in 1904. Today, the average American wolfs down two hundred hamburgers a year. McDonald's alone sells over 150 hamburgers per second in the U.S.

Snack Facts

WHY IS SODA REFERRED TO AS "POP"?

Flavored drinks are "carbonated" through the process of injecting carbon dioxide under pressure. This process was originated by Joseph Priestley in 1772 as an imitation of natural bubbly waters. The first sweetened carbonated drink was a ginger ale created by a Doctor Cantrall in Ireland in 1852. Originally, soft drinks were sold in glass bottles sealed with corks. Removing the cork from a bottle of soda, like removing the cork from a bottle of champagne today, released the pressure with an audible "pop."

WHY IS ICE CREAM TOPPED WITH CHOCOLATE OR FRUIT CALLED A "SUNDAE"?

A century ago, many parts of the U.S. had enacted strict blue laws designed to prohibit activities considered too sinful for the Sabbath. Amazingly, this often included the consumption of ice cream sodas. To attract customers without this favorite treat, a man named E.C. Berner poured chocolate syrup over a scoop of ice cream one day in 1890 in his Two Rivers, Wisconsin, establishment. Soon other parlors began offering ice cream with toppings which they advertised as "sodaless sodas." This concoction became very popular, and people began referring to it as a "Sunday." Later, owners of some ice cream parlors changed the spelling to "sundae" to convince people they could order the treat any day of the week.

WHY DO DOUGHNUTS HAVE HOLES?

The doughnut was invented in 1847 by a fifteen-year-old Camden, Maine, baker's apprentice named Hanson Crockett. Crockett noticed that his fried cakes were often uncooked in the center. When he cut out the middle, the problem was solved. Ring doughnuts soon became very popular.

WHY DOES POPCORN POP?

Popcorn is a special variety of Indian corn that has a much harder outer shell than ordinary varieties. When a kernel is heated, moisture in the pulp is converted to steam. The hard outer shell traps this steam for awhile, increasing the pressure inside. Eventually, pressure builds to the point where the shell disintegrates, producing a mini-explosion or "pop" that throws out the dry, white insides.

WHO INVENTED THE POPSICLE?

This frozen treat was first called an "epsicle," after a San Francisco man named Frank Epperson. Mr. Epperson left a glass of lemonade with a mixing stick on his windowsill one cold night in 1905. The next morning, he found a delicious and unexpected treat shaped like an icicle. As the idea gained popularity, some people began calling it an "ice lollypop." The two names merged into "popsicle."

WHO INVENTED THE POTATO CHIP?

In the summer of 1853, an American Indian named George Crum was working as a chef in an elegant hotel in fashionable Saratoga Springs, New York. One of his most popular dishes was thick-cut slices of potato known as "french fries." One guest, however, complained constantly that the fries were too thick. Unable to please him, Crum finally decided to get even by cutting slices of potato so thin that, when fried, the diner couldn't get a fork into them.

To Crum's astonishment, the guest raved about the thin-fried potatoes, and other guests soon clamored for them. They became so popular that Crum eventually quit his job and opened an entire restaurant devoted to what were now called "potato chips."

Other people copied the recipe, but until the 1920s, they were exclusively a northeastern snack. Then an enterprising salesman named Herman Lay filled his trunk with potato chips and began peddling them to stores all along the east coast. Lay's Potato Chips were the first national brand of what has now become one of America's favorite snacks.

WHERE DID THE PRETZEL COME FROM?

This charming story dates back to a monastery in northern Italy in 610 A.D. A medieval Italian monk decided to back a snack to reward children for memorizing prayers. He designed it in the crisscross shape to emulate the folded arms of children in prayer. The word "pretzels", itself, comes from a combination of the Latin *"prettiole,"* meaning "little gift," and *"bracciatelli,"* meaning "small arms."

What's a Fruit and What's a Vegetable?

What's the difference between a fruit, a berry, a bean and a vegetable? Before you answer, read the following descriptions of common products:

FRUITS

Botanists define a fruit as the ripened ovary of a flower and its contents. What we consider vegetable are often true fruits, such as olives, squash, cashews, wheat, corn, and rice. Oranges, lemons, tomatoes, watermelons, grapes, and cucumbers are technically considered berries. On the other hand, strawberries, raspberries, and blackberries are technically not berries at all, but rather collections of fruit. And to top it all off, only the inedible core of apples and pears is a fruit—the edible flesh is considered a "pome."

BANANA

Bananas do not grow on trees. Instead, the banana

plant is classified as the largest herb, and bananas are classified as berries. The stalk of a banana plant actually contains no wood — it's really leaf stalks wrapped together. Bananas grow in clumps of thirty to eighty at the end of a single stalk. Wild bananas are so full of seeds that they can't be eaten. The banana we buy in the grocery store is a hybrid seedless version that can only reproduce with human assistance.

COFFEE BEANS

Coffee beans aren't beans at all, but rather the pits of a cherrylike fruit. This fruit grows on treelike tropical shrubs that are often used for food.

NUTS

By definition a nut is a seed with a hard shell that does not split open until an embryo sprouts. Walnuts, pecans, acorns, filberts, and chestnuts are all true nuts. A peanut, however, is a member of the pea family. Coconuts, pistachios, and cashews are seeds of fruits, while almonds are the pits of a peach-like fruit.

Do You Eat Like a Bird and Drink Like a Fish?

We often say that a very thin person "eats like a bird." In truth, if you really ate like a bird, you'd soon die of obesity. The average bird consumes one-quarter to one-half its body weight in food every day. To match a robin's seventy-worm repast, you'd have to wolf down ten pounds of food over three meals.

And how much do fish drink? That depends on

their environment. Because seawater is more concentrated than their bodily fluids, saltwater fish lose fluid constantly through osmosis. So they take in an enormous quantity of water relative to their body weight. Freshwater fish, on the other hand, lose no fluid. If they took in any water at all, they'd drown. So you could be a teetotaler or a lush and still "drink like a fish."

Your Favorite Breakfast Cereals

When it comes to best-selling cereals, Wheaties isn't the champion—in fact, it doesn't even make the top ten. Americans eat more than twice as many bowls of the number-one cereal as they do of the number-two brand. The uncontested champ: Cheerios. Here's the top ten:

1. Cheerios
2. Corn Flakes
3. Frosted Flakes
4. Total
5. Rice Krispies
6. Raisin Bran
7. Chex
8. Cap'n Crunch
9. Shredded Wheat
10. Froot Loops

Why Don't We Eat Turkey Eggs?

Americans love turkey nearly as much as its fowl cousin, the chicken, so it would stand to reason that we'd also have an appetite for turkey eggs. Since turkey eggs are about twice the size as chicken eggs, a half dozen would go as far as a dozen of the eggs we now have in our refrigerators.

Unfortunately, turkeys refuse to cooperate in this scheme. The problem is that their eggs contain a lot less water than chicken eggs. So when they're cooked, they turn into something that's about the consistency of Silly Putty. Add to that the cost of turkey eggs — seventy-five cents a piece — and commercially you have a very unviable operation.

What about ostrich eggs? The size would be great for feeding a family reunion or your local football team. Our staff is checking on the palatability right now. In the meantime, we have to rely on our old standby, the hen.

People Who Eat People

The center sacrament of the Catholic Church is the Holy Eucharist, the symbolic ingestion of the body and blood of Jesus Christ in the form of bread and wine. This act is a more acceptable form of ritual cannibalism, which has been practiced by many people back to the dawn of history.

The purpose of ritual cannibalism (as opposed to

eating human flesh for survival) is to share in the deceased person's strength, virtue, and courage. There are two basic types of rituals. Exo-cannibalism is eating the flesh of people outside one's family or tribe. It was widely practiced by Australian aborigines, Maori tribe members, Eskimos, and many African tribes. Most desirable was the flesh of warriors, priests, or virgins.

Endo-cannibalism, on the other hand, involves eating the flesh of one's own relatives. This practice, a form of mourning, was common in Scandinavia and Ireland in ancient times. One Venezuelan tribe had the custom of carrying pieces of the flesh from a dead relative so that a nibble could be taken when grief became overwhelming.

Europeans were appalled by the practice of eating human flesh they encountered among natives of the New World. The word "cannibalism" comes from the Spanish word *"canibal,"* meaning "savage," which was applied to a flesh-eating tribe of the West Indies.

Except for a few tribes in remote reaches of New Guinea and Australia, cannibalism has largely disappeared. It exists primarily in fairy tales (e.g., the giant wants to eat Jack) and in the demented minds of serial killers such as Jeffrey Dahmer.

Speaking of Meat

Purchases of meat and fish account for about one-quarter of the food budget of the average American household. If you're an average adult American, every twelve months you consume:

79.2 pounds of beef
70.1 pounds of poultry (chicken and turkey)
62.0 pounds of pork
14.5 pounds of seafood
1.8 pounds of veal
1.4 pounds of lamb

When you eat out, twenty-two percent of you prefer fish, nineteen percent steak, seventeen percent shellfish, twelve percent roast beef, eleven percent chicken, three percent ham or pork, three percent veal, and one percent lamb. Of all people who order beef, twenty-nine percent like it rare, forty-two percent ask for medium, sixteen percent request medium rare or medium well-done, and thirteen percent prefer well-done.

Fried chicken is the first choice of diners-out, followed by baked and barbequed.

How Many Vegetables Do People Eat?

The average American consumed 197 pounds of vegetables in 1992: eighty-five pounds of fresh, ninety pounds of canned, and eighteen pounds of frozen. By type, the average consumption was:

Lettuce	27.4 pounds
Tomatoes	13.4 pounds
Onions	13.4 pounds
Cabbage	9.0 pounds
Celery	7.8 pounds
Corn	7.2 pounds

Carrots	6.3 pounds
Cucumbers	4.3 pounds
Peppers	3.6 pounds
Broccoli	1.8 pounds

Despite the health value of vegetables, only 3.7% of Americans classify themselves as vegetarians.

By the way, if you're interested, the average American eats 121 pounds of potatoes each year.

Your Restaurant Meals

According to the National Restaurant Association, more than one-third of all Americans purchase at least one meal away from home every day. On the average, you consumed one out of every five of your meals at a restaurant, and this dining pleasure accounted for two of every five dollars you spent on food. Young people ages eighteen to twenty-four dined out most frequently — an average of 250 meals per year.

About one-third of the meals purchased were take-out food. According to a Gallup Poll, most popular take-out items were:

Hamburgers	30%
Beverages	24%
French Fries	21%
Chicken	14%
Pizza	11%

On the average, Americans eat dinner in a restaurant five times per month. According to the National Restaurant Association, fifty-five percent of the adult diners prefer restaurants that feature good-old American cooking. Of those who favored ethnic fare, their favorite choices were:

Italian	36%
Chinese	23%
Mexican	20%
French	8%
German	6%
Greek	2%
Japanese	2%
Other	3%

According to the Gallup Report on Eating Out, about twelve percent of Americans charge their dinners on a credit card. And of all the people requesting "doggie bags" to take food home, only thirteen percent actually fed the food to a dog.

What You Drink

Big news in the beverage industry in the 1980s was that for the first time in history, the average American consumed more soft drinks than water during the course of a year. Of the 184 gallons of liquid annually downed by an adult, the liquids consumed were:

Soft drinks	50 gallons
Water	47 gallons
Bottled	5 gallons
Tap	42 gallons

Coffee	25 gallons
Beer	24 gallons
Milk	21 gallons
Fruit juice	11 gallons
Wine	3 gallons
Hard liquor	3 gallons

Almost two-thirds of all soft drinks consumed were cola drinks and thirteen percent were lemon-lime concoctions. Fifty-six percent of all soft drinks were consumed from cans, with the remainder split between bottles and fountain service.

Forty-four percent of men and forty-eight percent of women drank wine, with women accounting for fifty-eight percent of all wine purchases. Wine consumption averages 3.12 gallons per year per person, but those figures vary widely from state to state. Topping the list of imbibers are residents of Washington, D.C. who sip over nine gallons a year. On the other extreme, residents of Mississippi purchase less than one gallon during the year. Of all wine drinkers, sixty-two percent prefer white wine, twenty-two percent red wine, and sixteen percent rosé.

Fifty-seven percent of American men and fifty percent of women drink hard liquor, but men down eighty percent of all distilled spirits. It's no surprise that men make up the overwhelming majority of whiskey drinkers, while nine out of ten women favor mixed drinks over liquor served with water, soda, or on the rocks. The type of liquor preferred varies considerably with age and income: For example, rum is favored by twenty-eight percent of drinkers age twenty-four and under, but just nine percent of drinkers age forty and older. Of people who buy the most expensive brands, the most popular types are scotch, Canadian whiskey, bourbon, rum, and imported gin. The most popular mixed drinks, in order, are Bloody Mary, Whiskey Sour, Margarita, Daiquiri, and Tequila Sunrise.

What Do We Spend the Most Money On in the Grocery Store?

One of the most vicious wars waged under our noses each day is the competition for precious shelf space in America's grocery stores. Every additional foot of space can be translated into millions of dollars of sales and profits. The reason manufacturers issue three hundred billion coupons each year is to capture shelf space for new products or defend the already allocated spaces.

Who are the winners in this war? Following is a list of the top ten products in total sales in grocery stores:

Product	1991 Sales (in millions)
1. Marlboro cigarettes	$1,509
2. Coca-Cola Classic	$1,278
3. Pepsi	$1,222
4. Kraft cheese	$1,168
5. diet Coke	$ 996
6. Tide	$ 970
7. Campbell's soup	$ 964
8. Folgers coffee	$ 824
9. Winston cigarettes	$ 780
10. Tropicana	$ 685

Eight

Sports Trivia

How Did the America's Cup Get Its Name?

The world's most famous international yachting competition was not named for the United States of America. The trophy was originally the Hundred Guineas Cup, the grand prize offered by the British Royal Yacht Squadron, which sponsored a series of races during the London Exposition of 1851. The winner, which triumphed over twenty-four challengers, was a yacht named *America*. The owners took the trophy across the Atlantic to the New York Yacht Club and renamed the competition the America's Cup, in honor of their champion yacht.

What's the National Sport of Canada?

If you answer "hockey," you're wrong. In 1867, the Canadian Parliament officially handed the title of Canadian National Sport to lacrosse. This rugged game was originated by Native American tribes, whose contests often lasted days and resulted in injuries and even deaths. Early French settlers thought the netted sticks used by the Indians looked like the hooked staffs, or "croziers," carried by Catholic bishops. So they named the game *"la crosse."* It stuck, and it's still popular north of our border.

When Were the First Baseball Cards Issued?

More than a century ago, long before Surgeon General's warnings, tobacco companies were among the most aggressive companies in marketing their products. In 1887, a firm called Goodwin & Company came up with the idea of taking pictures of baseball stars, gluing them onto $1\frac{1}{2}'' \times 2\frac{1}{2}''$ pieces of cardboard, and inserting them as premiums into packages of cigarettes with such exotic names as Old Judge, Gypsy Queen, and Dog's Head. This use of baseball cards was popular until the mid-1890s, when the American Tobacco Company grabbed such a large market share that they decided they no longer had to spend money on promotion. However, the monopoly didn't last. By 1909, dozens of companies again turned to baseball cards to spur sales.

Baseball cards and bubble gum didn't become partners until the mid-1930s, when gum manufacturers combined rubber tree products with gum to create the elasticity necessary to blow bubbles. Teaming a slab of gum with a baseball card was a natural marketing strategy. With the exception of the period between 1941-1948 (when natural resources like rubber, paper, and ink were reserved for the war effort), bubble gum manufacturers have been the major producers of baseball cards.

However, gum and tobacco have not had an exclusive hold on sports cards. Baseball cards have been issued in connection with caramel, cheese, chocolate, cookies, Cracker Jacks, magazines, ice cream, milk, soft drinks, tea, meat products, dog food, potato chips, cereal, Jell-O, beef jerky, snack cakes, and macaroni.

Over the last two decades, baseball card collecting has become a big business, with the values of some rare cards soaring into the tens of thousands of dollars. The most valuable card of all dates back to 1909, when a tobacco company issued a set of cards featuring five hundred players. One future Hall of Famer, Honus Wagner, objected to his likeness being used. The most widely circulated story is that Wagner's objection was based on his religious abhorance of tobacco; in reality, he may have been more upset that he wasn't getting paid. However, the card was pulled, and very few got into circulation. Today, an estimated fifty survive, and the price for one, depending on condition, ranges upward of $100,000.

Why Are Basketball Players Called "Cagers"?

In the early days of the sport, basketball courts were surrounded by metal or cloth netting. The purpose: to prevent the ball from going into the crowd. And because these spectators occasionally got a bit rowdy, the barrier served the dual purpose of preventing the spectators from throwing things at the referees and players and keeping them from physically charging onto the court. Because basketball was played in what was essentially a cage, basketball players became known as "cagers."

Why Is the Georgetown Basketball Team Known as the Hoyas?

If you're a college basketball fan, you've probably wondered, "What in heaven's name is a Hoya?" It sounds like some Central American lizard. The real derivation is even more bizarre. Georgetown students, a century ago, were evidently a very literate lot. The school baseball team used to be known as the Stonewalls. For some unknown reason, students combined the Greek word *"hoya,"* which means "what," with the Latin word *"saxa,"* which means "rocks," to produce the cheer, *"Hoya saxa!",* or "What rocks!" Eventually, the phrase was shortened to *"Hoya."* So if you root for John Thompson's team, you're rooting for the Georgetown "Whats"!

Why Is A Left-handed Pitcher Called A "Southpaw"?

Covering baseball daily for a newspaper can sometimes be a tedious job, and sportswriters' minds sometimes wander. One day in the 1880s, Chicago sportswriter Finley Peter Dunne, who later became a famous humorist, happened to reflect upon the geographic orientation of the baseball field. The home plate faced west, center field east, first base south, and third base north. A left-handed pitcher was on the mound, and Dunne noticed that his hand (or paw) was facing south. In his article on that day's game, he referred to the pitcher as a "southpaw."

The name stuck. Unfortunately, no one has ever called a right-handed pitcher a "northpaw."

Why Are Strikeouts In Baseball Called "Ks"?

This one is more logical. In the early days of baseball, fans and officials developed the same shorthand system of scorekeeping we use today. "E" stood for "error," "1B" for a single, "W" for "walk," etc. Scorekeepers used "S" for "sacrifice," so it couldn't also serve as the symbol for "strikeout." So they settled on another prominent consonant in the word, "K."

Why Is A Score of Zero in Tennis Called "Love"?

No, it doesn't have a romantic origin. Instead, it's French. Evidently, the French use the slang expression "goose egg" for zero, just as we do. In French, "egg" is *"oeuf,"* which is pronounced "oove." It was corrupted to "love," which sounds a whole lot better, anyway.

Why Is There A Seventh-inning Stretch in Baseball?

The most widely circulated story about this custom is that President William Howard Taft was attending a Washington Senator game one day. Duty called, and he got up to go back to the White House in the middle of the seventh inning. Out of respect, the rest of the spectators rose, giving rise to the custom. The story is nice, but it's probably not true.

More believable is that the custom dates back to 1882, when the Manhattan College baseball coach noticed that fans got restless during the games and began asking them to stand up and stretch in the middle of the seventh inning. Manhattan College played exhibition games at the Polo Grounds, home field of the New York Giants, and the custom eventually spread to professional fans.

Where Did the Golf Terms "Bogey" and "Birdie" Come From?

Today, the word "bogey" means completing a hole in a score one over par, while "birdie" means completing a hole in a score one under par. The word "bogey" comes from a popular English song titled "Colonel Bogey." For some reason, a golfer who completed a hole with the lowest score became known as "Colonel Bogey." Eventually, the term was shortened to "bogey," and came to mean completing a hole in the required number of strokes. Since Americans already used the word "par," they used "bogey" to mean "one over par," and it became standard in the sport.

In the early 1900s, "bird" was an American slang term for something that was rare. Golfers completing a hole one under par began calling their achievement "a bird," and that soon became "birdie."

Why Is the Distance of the Marathon Twenty-six Miles, 385 Yards?

The term "marathon" for a long-distance running event dates way back to 490 B.C., when the Greeks established a running event in their Olympics to honor the legendary achievement of a soldier who ran from the Plains of Marathon to Athens (a distance of twenty-two miles, 1,470 yards) to announce victory. The soldier then collapsed and died. In the ancient Olympics, marathons were run at distances of approximately twenty-five miles.

When the modern Olympic Games were started in 1896, the marathon was run at various lengths. Then, at the London Olympics of 1908, the British decided that the marathon course would run from Windsor Castle to the royal box at London Stadium. That distance was twenty-six miles, 385 yards, which became the standard length of a marathon.

Why Are There Ten Pins in Bowling?

Bowling is one of the most ancient of mankind's recreations. We know that the ancient Egyptians bowled, and there is some evidence that early humans who lived in caves also threw stones at objects for sport. The Polynesians participated in this activity by aiming at an object at the end of a sixty-foot alley, the same length as our modern bowling alley.

The game we play today probably is derived from a fourteenth century German game in which a stone was thrown at a bottle-shaped wooden object called a *"kegel"* (hence, bowlers are known as "keglers"). The Dutch eventually modified the sport by using nine bottle-shaped pins.

The Dutch settlers brought their nine-pin game to America. Although the game was originally played outdoors, indoor alleys were eventually built, and a great deal of money was wagered on the outcome. Some states, such as Connecticut, outlawed nine-pin bowling to stop the gambling. To skirt the law, the bowlers added a tenth pin, and that became the standard we use today.

Why Are Golf Courses Called "Links" and Why Are Bunkers Filled with Sand?

Golf originated in the seaside areas of Scotland, which were covered with scrub brush and sand. The only areas that were green were the fairways and greens. From a distance, the holes looked like they were "linked" together by ribbons of green. So they became known as "links."

These early golf courses shared the land with grazing sheep. Because the wind often howls in Scotland, the sheep would gather in natural depressions to graze. Sand eventually drifted in, and these depressions became natural hazards for the players.

Nine

The Animal Kingdom

Which Is Which?

What's the difference between a frog and a toad? Between an Asian rhinoceros and an Indian rhinoceros? If you don't know, here's a guide that will make you an expert on your next trip to the zoo.

FROG AND TOAD
Frogs have smooth, moist skin and are great jumpers. Toads have rough, dry skin and move in short, clumsy hops.

INSECTS AND BUGS

A bug is a kind of insect that has larger front wings than rear wings, and its sucking mouth parts in the front of its head.

ALLIGATORS AND CROCODILES

An alligator's snout is rounded, with the width at the tip nearly the same as the width at the eyes. The snout of a crocodile narrows sharply from the eyes to the nose.

AFRICAN AND ASIAN ELEPHANTS

African elephants are much larger and sport huge, floppy ears. African elephants have three toes on their hind feet, while Asian elephants have four.

ONE-HUMPED AND TWO-HUMPED CAMELS

The one-humped camel, called a dromedary, is native to India and North Africa. The two-humped camel, called a Bactrian, is native to China, Turkey, and Mongolia.

OLD WORLD AND NEW WORLD MONKEYS

Old World monkeys, natives of Asia and Africa, can not use their tails for grasping. New World monkeys, found in Central and South America, have grasping tails.

AFRICAN AND INDIAN RHINOCEROS

The Indian rhinoceros has one horn, while the African rhinoceros has two.

How Did Hamsters Become Popular Pets?

Ever see a wild hamster? You probably never have, because the species is found only in a small area of Syria around the town of Aleppo (which is why the species is known as the Syrian golden hamster). Although Western zoologists first encountered the little rodents in the late 1700s, little attention was paid to them until 1930, when a scientist named Israel Aharoni captured a mother and eleven babies. Upset by the disruption in her nursing routine, the mother became crazed and killed one of the babies. That vicious act in turn enraged one of Aharoni's employees, who promptly drowned the mother in a bottle of cyanide.

So Aharoni was forced to hand feed the helpless remaining young. He soon discovered that hamsters thrived in captivity and were very well-suited for laboratory experiments. Hamsters were shipped first to Europe, then, in 1938, to the United States. After World War II, they became popular pets.

Who Owns Pets?

About six of every ten American households contains at least one pet. According to a University of Chicago study, eighty-eight percent of pet owners said their pet was "extremely" or "very" important to them. Nearly eighty percent said that, at times, their pet was their closest companion, and almost half kept pictures of their pet in their wallet. Another indication of how important pets are to us is the fact that the average supermarket devotes 240-linear feet to pet food and products, the most of any product line.

DOGS

About thirty-seven percent of American households own forty-six million dogs, an average of 1.44 dogs per dog-owning household. Most likely to own dogs were households with four or more people, high-income households, or households with children.

By far, the largest number of people owned mixed breed dogs (thirty-one percent). Next most popular were German shepherds (seven percent), golden retrievers (six percent), and Labrador retrievers (six percent). How much does it cost to own a dog? One New York veterinarian figured out that the average dog costs about nine cents per hour over an eleven-year-life span.

CATS

Americans own about as many cats as dogs, but only twenty-six percent of households have cats. That means an average of 2.03 cats per cat-owning household. The cat population is expected to rise by about ten million over the next ten years. Cat-owning households are more likely to be childless, more likely to have both husband and wife working, and more likely to be in a big city rather than a suburb.

BIRDS

About fifteen percent of American households owned twenty-seven million birds, with an average of a little under two birds per household. The most common bird by far was the parakeet, which lives about seven years.

FISH

About twelve percent of households own an average of twenty-five fish each. That means a whopping 250,000,000 fish swimming around in American aquariums.

OTHER PETS

Hamsters, gerbils, rabbits, and reptiles each inhabit between 1% and 2% of American households. Among these, reptile ownership is the fastest growing hobby.

How Did the Legend That Storks Bring Babies Begin?

This children's tale began in Germany and Scandinavia several centuries ago. Every spring, white storks returned to northern Europe from their winter habitat in Africa. They nested on rooftops near chimneys to raise their young. People began to believe that storks were a symbol of fertility, and choosing a rooftop to nest upon meant good luck for the inhabitants. To avoid telling small children the facts of life, parents would explain that storks brought babies, but the mother needed bed rest afterwards because the birds bite.

Storks, by the way, are terrible parents. If they don't

have enough food, they often abandon their young or even eat them.

Why Do Cats Love Catnip?

Catnip was a common European herb that was brought to the United States by early settlers, who grew it for its medicinal qualities. They believed catnip tea eased intestinal cramps and increased menstrual flow. Chewing catnip leaves was a toothache remedy.

To cats, however, catnip is intoxicating. Because of their particular blood chemistry, they get "high" from the oil that is released when catnip leaves are bruised or broken. The purpose of the oil is to prevent insects from eating the leaves, but that defense mechanism wasn't evolved with cats in mind.

Rumors to the contrary, catnip has absolutely no hallucinogenic effects on humans.

Are Woolly Bears Weather-wise?

There probably isn't a weatherman who hasn't been asked "How come a woolly bear knows when the winter will be harsh . . . and you don't?" What they're really saying is, "Weatherman, how come you're dumber than an insect?"

The truth is, though, that woolly bears aren't smarter than meteorologists (though they may be cuter). The width of the stripes on these caterpillars' backs (folklore says that if the brown stripe is wider than the black stripe, the winter will be long and harsh) is determined by a combination of genetics and the environmental conditions when the insect is growing. Scientific studies have shown absolutely no correlation between the width of the stripes and future weather.

But laying the woolly bear myth to bed doesn't mean that you should dismiss all weather sayings and folklore. As I have mentioned previously, in the thousands of years before the development of sophisticated instruments and supercomputers, humans had to depend on their keen powers of observation for clues to the upcoming weather. These observations produced many nuggets of wisdom that are still useful to us today.

Of course, along with the wisdom is a lot of superstition. I have always found separating fact from folklore to be a fascinating activity. You'll enjoy discovering which weather sayings have some basis in truth and which are fiction.

ANIMALS

* Swallows fly high, clear blue sky
  Swallows fly low, rain we shall know.

* Fish bite just before it rains.

* Before a storm, cows will lie down and refuse to go out to pasture.

* Cats will lick themselves constantly before a storm.

* It will be a cold, snowy winter if:

— Squirrels accumulate huge stores of nuts.
— Beavers build heavier lodges than usual.
— Hair on bears and horses is thick early in season.
— The breastbone of a fresh-cooked turkey is dark purple.

Many ancient societies worshiped animals, and an extension of that worship was the belief that certain animals had the ability to predict the future. Although such prognostication techniques as examining the entrails of a goat have been long abandoned, many people still accept the idea that animals are somehow "smarter" about nature than we are. That's why weather sayings and folklore involving animals are so prevalent.

Which of these beliefs are true? To understand, compare some fish, animals, and birds to weather instruments such as barometers, thermometers, hygrometers, and weather vanes. Because most species are very vulnerable to environmental changes, they may be sensitive to slight changes in air pressure, humidity, temperature, and wind direction that we humans can't detect. For example, swallows flying unusually low indicates that the air pressure is dropping, in the same way that the level of mercury in a barometer falls. Because a drop in air pressure can be a sign of approaching inclement weather, low-flying swallows is a sign that the chance of rain has increased.

Falling air pressure may affect the digestive systems of cows, making them less willing to go to pasture. Static electricity in the air before a storm may increase the grooming activities of cats. When seagulls stay close to shore, so do fishermen, who have noticed that such avian behavior often precedes storms. The cawing of crows, the honking of geese, and the calls of other birds become louder and more frequent as low-pressure areas approach. There's evidence that deer and elk react to wind and air pressure changes by coming down from mountains and seeking shelter. Many species from rabbits to rattlesnakes to certain kinds of fish may feed more frenetically before a storm, during which they seek shelter.

These creatures are not making weather predictions; they are simply reacting to existing environmental conditions. If you're interested in what the weather will be like in three months, you'll have about the same luck asking your thermometer as you would checking out the food supply in a squirrel's nest or the size of a beaver's lodge. A bear or a horse may grow a heavier coat if November is especially cold, but that doesn't necessarily mean the entire winter will be harsh — December 1989 was the fourth coldest December in U.S. history, while January 1990 was the warmest in history. If you're interested in finding out if squirrels or horses have any psychic power to predict the weather, you'll have to consult your Ouija board.

Topping the list of most bizarre animal folklore is the belief that animal tissue retains the ability to predict weather long after the creature's death. The Apache Indians believed that certain patterns that formed in bear fat were signs of certain types of approaching weather. Getting a bear to cooperate is just the first of many problems with this forecasting theory.

INSECTS, WORMS, AND OTHER
CREEPY, CRAWLY THINGS

* You can find out the temperature by counting the number of times a cricket chirps in fifteen seconds and adding forty.
* When spiders weave their webs by noon, fine weather is coming soon.
* Flies and gnats swarm and bite before a storm.
* If wasps build their nests high, the winter will be long and harsh.

In 1851, Dr. George Merryweather arrived at London's Great Exhibition with his revolutionary new weather-predicting invention, which consisted of twelve leeches, twelve jars, and a bell. When the leeches became active, they would trip a switch that rang a bell that warned of an approaching storm. Merryweather urged the British government to establish a network of leech-activated bells along the entire length of that country's coastline.

The good doctor's suggestion wasn't implemented, but he also wasn't laughed out of town. For hundreds of years, people had related leech activity to the arrival of foul weather—with some justification. Insects, as well as other animals, are extremely sensitive to changes in their environments. When the air pressure drops, flying insects from flies to mosquitoes are much more active and stay closer to the ground. Cicadas hum loudly in dry weather, but can't vibrate their wings when the humidity is very high. Bees have difficulty carrying pollen when the humidity is very high, which makes them buzz irritably. A number of scientific studies have shown that the frequency of cricket chirps is directly related to temperature (if you're interested in the temperature at cricket-level).

But even though weatherpeople may bug you, you can't turn instead to any insect for long-range forecasts, whether it's a wasp or a woolly bear.

Why Are Piggy Banks Shaped Like Pigs?

In ancient times, a lump of the clay used for molding bowls, jars, and other such utensils was known as a *"pygg."* Because all money was coins in those days, people kept these coins in bowls that eventually became known as pygg bowl banks.

We now move sometime later in history when the word *pygg* had fallen out of fashion. The legend is that someone placed an order with a potter for *pygg* bowl banks. He took the word to mean swine and fashioned several ceramic banks shaped like pigs. That shape soon became customary.

Funny Animal Stories

* A forty-nine-year-old West Palm Beach, Florida, woman was arrested when undercover cops posing as house hunters found several marijuana plants growing in pots on her back porch. The woman's defense: The illegal plants were the only food her pet iguana Kiko would eat. After the plants were taken away, the lizard went on a hunger strike and died. Prosecutors dropped the charges because they determined that the police search had been illegal.

* Runaway pets usually turn up in a few days. But in the case of Myrtle the Turtle, a forty-five-year-old desert tortoise who moves very slowly, the process of recovery took a lot longer. Myrtle, who evidently had a yen for rambling, ran away from her Long Beach, California, owner in 1982. She was on the lam for ten years before she was spotted strolling down the sidewalk — nearly two hundred miles from home. Because desert tortoises are a threatened species, Myrtle had been registered with the state's Department of Fish and Game and wore a numbered tag that allowed authorities to return her to her owner. But she was mum on how she'd spent her time on her little stroll.

* A woman rented a car from Avis in Melbourne, Florida, and drove almost two thousand miles to her parents' home near Rochester, New York. As she stopped the car, a 4½-foot python slithered out from under the dash and wrapped itself around the steering wheel. Turns out the snake had been left in the car by the previous renter. We'd like to know: How absentminded do you have to be to forget a 4½-foot python?

* A Long Island, New York, duck farm that supplied duck livers for the *foi gras* served in many of New York's most prestigious restaurants was raided by the Suffolk County District Attorney's office and charged with animal abuse. According to authorities, the farm workers shoved a foot-long metal tube down the ducks' throats three times a day and force-fed huge amounts of food with compressed air. Frequently, too much

food was used, and the ducks exploded. Employees were awarded a bonus if they exploded less than fifty ducks per month. Many ducks got so fat they were unable to walk, and the top of their bills was cut off so they couldn't eat or drink normally.

* Wildlife experts in Denver, Colorado, called a news conference to demonstrate the first operation to implant a birth control device in a beaver. Apparently, a beaver population explosion has been causing turmoil in the Denver suburbs. Anyway, the television cameras were rolling until embarrassed experts stopped the procedure, explaining sheepishly that the beaver undergoing the implant turned out to be a male.

Ten

Celebrity Trivia

Weird First Names

While many celebrities change their names completely, others simply drop a first name they dislike. After reading the following list, you'll understand why these decisions were made.

Celebrity	Real First Name
* Ed Asner	Yitzak
* Gene Autry	Orvon
* Warren Beatty	Henry
* Joan Caulfield	Beatrice

* Mac Davis	Morris
°* Faye Dunaway	Dorothy
* John (Jackie) Gleason	Herbert
* Van Heflin	Emmet
* Marie Osmond	Olive
* Gregory Peck	Eldred
* Jane Russell	Ernestine
* Neil Simon	Marvin
* Bobby Vinton	Stanley
* Bruce Willis	Walter
* Flip Wilson	Clerow

Famous High School Dropouts

We all endlessly preach to our kids about the importance of a formal education. That's why you should never, ever let them see this list of people who succeeded despite having dropped out of high school — a list that includes two famous network news anchors and several best-selling authors.

Danny Aiello	Rod McKuen
Richard Avedon	Dean Martin
Sonny Bono	Elaine May
David Bowie	Roger Moore
Michael Caine	Al Pacino
George Carlin	Sidney Poitier
John Chancellor	Richard Pryor
Jackie Collins	Anthony Quinn
Sean Connery	Harold Robbins
Carrie Fisher	Rod Steiger

Michael J. Fox
James Garner
Cary Grant
Gene Hackman
Peter Jennings

Danny Thomas
Randy Travis
Peter Ustinov
Robert Wagner

Celebrity Jailbirds

Celebrities aren't saints, as all of you who read the papers know. While a lot of scandals involve gossip, below is a verified list of famous people who have spent at least one night in the slammer.

Roseanne Arnold
James Bakker
Chuck Berry
James Brown
Truman Capote
Johnny Cash
David Crosby
Tony Danza
Brian DePalma
Phil Donahue
Farrah Fawcett
Cyndi Garvey
Jerry Hall

Richard Harris
Stacy Keach
Evel Knievel
Sophia Loren
Robert Mitchum
Paul Newman
Nick Nolte
Sean Penn
Pete Seeger
O.J. Simpson
Ike Turner
Mae West
Dave Winfield

Celebrity Real Names

Who's Alphonso D'Abruzzo? One of America's all-time favorite television actors. But he may not have had much of a career if he hadn't changed his name to Alan Alda. Following is a list of some other famous people and their real names.

* Jane Alexander	Jane Quigley
* Woody Allen	Allen Stewart Konigsberg
* June Allyson	Ella Geisman
* Elizabeth Arden	Florence Nightingale Graham
* Eve Arden	Eunice Quedens
* Desi Arnaz	Desiderio Alberto Arnaz de Acha, II
* Fred Astaire	Frederick Austerlitz
* Pat Benatar	Patricia Andrejewski
* Jack Benny	Benjamin Kubelsky
* Robert Blake	Michael Gubitosi
* David Bowie	David Robert Jones
* Morgan Brittany	Suzanne Cupito
* Charles Bronson	Charles Buchinski
* Mel Brooks	Melvin Kaminsky
* George Burns	Nathan Birnbaum
* Nicholas Cage	Nicholas Coppola
* Michael Caine	Maurice J. Micklewhite
* Dyan Cannon	Samile Diane Friesen
* Kate Capshaw	Kathy Sue Nail
* Chevy Chase	Cornelius Crane Chase
* Eric Clapton	Cedric Clapp
* Andrew Dice Clay	Andrew Silverstein
* Robert Conrad	Conrad Robert Falk
* David Copperfield	David Kotkin
* Elvis Costello	Declan Patrick McManus

* Tom Cruise	Thomas Cruise Mapother, IV
* Tony Curtis	Bernard Schwartz
* Rodney Dangerfield	Jacob Cohen
* Tony Danza	Anthony Iadanza
* Doris Day	Doris von Kappelhoff
* Jimmy Dean	Seth Ward
* Patrick Dennis	Edward Everett Tanner, III
* John Denver	Henry John Deutschendorf, Jr.
* Bo Derek	Mary Cathleen Collins
* Bo Diddley	Elias McDaniels-Bates
* Phyllis Diller	Phyllis Driver
* Kirk Douglas	Issur Danielovitch Demsky
* Bob Dylan	Robert Zimmerman
* Chad Everett	Raymond Lee Cramton
* Morgan Fairchild	Patsy Ann McClenny
* Gerald R. Ford	Leslie Lynch King, Jr.
* Jodie Foster	Alicia Christian Foster
* Redd Foxx	John Elroy Sanford
* Vincent Gardenia	Vincent Scognamiglio
* Judy Garland	Frances Gumm
* James Garner	James Scott Bumgarner
* Crystal Gayle	Brenda Gayle Webb
* Bobbie Gentry	Roberta Streeter
* Estelle Getty	Estelle Scher
* Whoopi Goldberg	Caryn Johnson
* Cary Grant	Alexander Archibald Leach
* Lee Grant	Lyova Haskell Rosenthal

* Paul Harvey	Pauly Harvey Aurandt
* Rita Hayworth	Margarita Cansino
* Pee-Wee Herman	Paul Rubenfeld
* Hulk Hogan	Terry Jean Bollette
* William Holden	William Franklin Beedle, Jr.
* Harry Houdini	Ehrich Weiss
* Rock Hudson	Roy Scherer, Jr.
* Engelbert Humperdinck	Arnold Gerry Dorsey
* Billy Idol	William Board
* Rick James	James Johnson
* Elton John	Reginald Kenneth Dwight
* Don Johnson	Donald Wayne
* Boris Karloff	William Henry Pratt
* Danny Kaye	David Daniel Kominski
* Diane Keaton	Diane Hall
* Michael Keaton	Michael Douglas
* Chaka Khan	Yvette Marie Stevens
* Alan King	Irwin Alan Kniberg
* Larry King	Larry Zeigler
* Martin Luther King, Jr.	Michael Luther King, Jr.
* Ben Kingsley	Krishna Bhanji
* Nastassja Kinski	Nastassja Naksyznyski
* Ted Knight	Tadeus Wladyslaw Konopka
* Patti LaBelle	Patricia Louise Holte
* Ann Landers	Esther Pauline Friedman
* Michael Landon	Eugene Maurice Orowitz
* Carol Lawrence	Carol Marie Laraia

* Steve Lawrence	Sidney Leibowitz
* Bruce Lee	Lee Yuen Kam
* Spike Lee	Shelton Lee
* Jerry Lewis	Joseph Levitch
* Little Richard	Richard Wayne Penniman
* Sophia Loren	Sofia Scicolone
* Madonna	Madonna Louise Ciccone
* Lee Majors	Harvey Lee Yeary, II
* Malcolm X	Malcolm Little
* Dean Martin	Dino Crocetti
* Jackie Mason	Jacob Masler
* Meat Loaf	Marvin Lee Adair
* Joni Mitchell	Roberta Joan Anderson
* Eddie Money	Edward Mahoney
* Marilyn Monroe	Norma Jean Mortenson or Baker
* Yves Montand	Yvo Montand Livi
* Demi Moore	Demi Gynes
* Rita Moreno	Rosita Dolores Alverio
* Mike Nichols	Michael Igor Peschkowsky
* Chuck Norris	Carlos Ray Norris
* Patti Page	Clara Ann Fowler
* Johnny Paycheck	Don Lytle
* Minnie Pearl	Sarah Ophelia Colley Cannon
* Bernadette Peters	Bernadette Lazzara
* Michelle Philips	Holly Michelle Gilliam
* Christopher Plummer	Arthur Christopher Ormf
* Iggy Pop	James Jewel Osterburg

* Stefanie Powers	Stefania Zofia Federkiewicz
* Prince	Prince Rogers Nelson
* Joan Rivers	Joan Sandra Molinsky
* Harold Robbins	Francis Kane
* Edward G. Robinson	Emanuel Goldenberg
* Ginger Rogers	Virginia Katherine McMath
* Roy Rogers	Leonard Slye
* Winona Ryder	Winona Horowitz
* Soupy Sales	Milton Hines
* Susan Sarandon	Susan Abigail Tomaling
* Jane Seymour	Joyce Penelope Frankenberg
* Omar Sharif	Michael Shalhoub
* Martin Sheen	Ramon Estevez
* Dinah Shore	Fanny Rose Shore
* Beverly Sills	Belle Miriam Silverman
* Joseph Stalin	Iosif Dzhugashvili
* Sting	Gordon Matthew Sumner
* Danny Thomas	Muzyad Yakhoob, later Arnos Jacobs
* Randy Travis	Randy Traywick
* Tina Turner	Annie Mae Bullock
* Twiggy	Leslie Hornby
* Conway Twitty	Harold Lloyd Jenkins
* Abigail Van Buren	Pauline Esther Friedman
* Lindsay Wagner	Lindsay Jean Ball
* Muddy Waters	McKinley Morganfield
* John Wayne	Marion Michael Morrison

* Sigourney Weaver   Susan Weaver
* Gene Wilder   Jerome Silberman
* Stevie Wonder   Steveland Judkins
* Natalie Wood   Natasha Gurdin
* Tammy Wynette   Wynette Pugh

Famous Twins

Are two kings better than one king? Rock-and-roll fans may have had to ponder that problem if Elvis's twin had survived birth. Then again, maybe his twin wouldn't have been able to sing a note. Below are the famous half of twins:

Mario Andretti   Liberace
Jose Canseco   Laraine Newman
Montgomery Clift   Lori Singer
Laraine Day   Ed Sullivan
John Elway   Kiefer Sutherland
Jerry Falwell   Jim Thorpe
Jerry Hall   Paul Tsongas
William Randolph   Clint Walker
Hearst   Billy Dee Williams
Laura Z. Hobson

Making Babies

Anyone who didn't realize that Mia Farrow had a regular posse of kids (eight, to be exact) must have been holed up in a Himalayan monastery for the last couple of years. But you may be surprised to discover that Mia is far from first on the "who's got the most kids" celebrity list. The champ is diminutive Mickey Rooney, who's fathered a whopping eleven offspring. Others who've had a half dozen or more include:

* Dennis Day   10
* Dick Gregory   10
* Marlon Brando   9
* Glen Campbell   9
* Michael Landon   9
* Danielle Steel   9
* Frankie Avalon   8
* Al Hirt   8
* Norman Mailer   8
* Dean Martin   7
* Harry Reasoner   7
* Muhammmad Ali   6
* Charles Bronson   6
* Jerry Lewis   6
* Loretta Lynn   6
* Paul Newman   6
* Sidney Poitier   6
* Jason Robards, Jr.   6
* Roy Rogers   6
* Andy Rooney   6
* George C. Scott   6

Celebrity Scandal

Why do we all love gossip, especially celebrity gossip? Probably because it makes us feel closer to famous people when they demonstrate the same human weaknesses as we do. But analyzing gossip isn't as much fun as dishing dirt. So let's take a look at some scandals involving famous names:

BUSH, GEORGE

The White House budget for travel in 1992 was a modest $29,000. But the real cost, according to Congressional sources, is close to a whopping $60 million. Every time the former president decided to fly to Maine for the weekend, Air Force One rolled up, a 747 that cost $26,000 an hour to operate. Behind the president's plane, at $9,000 an hour, was a cargo plane containing the president's bullet-proof limousine, Secret Service "war wagons," and a White House communications car. In the interest of the economy, don't you think Bush could have played golf in the Washington area for a few weekends?

CLAPTON, ERIC

Stories about the tragic death of the singer's four-year-old son, who fell four hundred feet from the window of his mother's Manhattan apartment building, indicated that the boy was Clapton's only child. But a British inquest into the boy's death brought to light the fact that Clapton was the father of a seven-year-old girl by a married woman who lives on the Caribbean island of Montserrat. The woman later reunited with her husband, and together they raise the little blond girl.

CURTIS, TONY

A twenty-eight-year-old female former employee of a Honolulu art gallery, from which Tony Curtis bought paintings, filed a lawsuit against the actor charging sexual harassment. The woman said that she was hired by the gallery to assist Curtis at his home, where he allegedly harassed her. She claims she was fired a year later because she resisted. Curtis denied the allegation.

DAHMER, JEFFREY

Of all the horrors committed by this serial killer, perhaps the most bizarre came to light this year when evidence surfaced that he attempted to turn some of his victims into zombies before killing them. Dahmer drugged the victims, then performed lobotomies by drilling into their skulls and pouring various fluids inside. When his experiments failed, he then strangled his victims and dissected them.

GABOR, ZSA ZSA

Ever wonder how Zsa Zsa lives the life-style of the rich and famous while tooling around getting in accidents with her Rolls-Royce? Well, her eighth hubby, Prince Frederic von Anhalt, evidently makes a nice living as a dealer in European titles, like Prince, Count, etc. How can a title be sold? you ask. According to von Anhalt, "Most of the titles are transferred through adoption, where the prince, baron, or whatever adopts the buyer, giving him or her a title." In other cases, von Anhalt says his clients, "can marry and then get divorced right after and keep the title." Now, with all the hunger and suffering in the world, doesn't this seem like a great way for people to spend their money?

Zsa Zsa's autobiography *One Lifetime is Not Enough* contains the following interesting statistics:

—Number of marriage proposals she's turned

down: 4
- Number of sexual proposals she's turned down: 12
- Number of priests turned down: 1
- Number of Warren Beatty propositions: 1 (she declined)
- Number of times she slept with Frank Sinatra so he would move his Cadillac out of her driveway: 1
- Number of pages devoted to her 5-year marriage to Michael O'Hara: 1
- Number of times diamonds are mentioned: 55

HITLER, ADOLF

This may come as a complete shock to you, but the exalted Fuhrer of the Third Reich, leader of the noble Aryan race, evidently didn't consider taking a bath as one of his obligations. Said former silent-screen actress Lina Basquette, commenting on Hitler's unsuccessful attempt to seduce her, "Maybe if I hadn't been so fastidious I might have changed history. But, oh, that body odor of his."

JACKSON, MICHAEL

The eccentric entertainer set U.S.-African relations back one hundred years by his behavior on a trip to the Ivory Coast. Jackson, evidently terrified by the less than perfect living conditions, wore a surgical mask in public and refused to shake hands or touch anyone. The impact of the visit was summed up by a commentator for an Ivory Coast newspaper, as follows:

The American sacred beast took it upon himself to remind us we are underdeveloped, impure, our air is polluted, infested with germs. And it's not this mutant genius, this voluntary mutant, this recreated being, bleached, neither white nor black, neither man nor woman, so delicate, so frail, who will inhale it.

KENNEDY, TED

Kennedy, who has been the focus of more scandals than any other political figure over the last two decades, bid adieu to single life in 1992 when he wed Washington lawyer Victoria Reggie. The wedding, however, was a civil ceremony: Boston's Bernard Cardinal Law issued a pronouncement banning a church wedding because Senator Kennedy is still married to his first wife Joan in the eyes of the church. When Kennedy married, he was considered estranged from the church and is unable to accept Holy Communion. Senator Kennedy, however, seemed to bear up under the burden of another sin quite well.

LED ZEPPELIN

In his book *Stairway to Heaven: Led Zeppelin Uncensored,* Richard Cole, the band's tour manager, describes some "fishy stories" that have been the subject of rumors for years. One story, which Cole calls the "Shark Episode," spawned rumors that a female fan had been tied to a bed in Seattle's Edgewater Inn and that "a shark had been used to penetrate her." According to Cole, the truth is that a seventeen-year-old female redhead had asked to be tied up, and Cole had used a red snapper to provide stimulation. He also writes that he and another member of the group persuaded two groupies to take a nude bath with four octopuses which, he says, "somehow instinctively knew where to place their tentacles" to send the girls into ecstasy. And you thought business trips were boring!

LUNDEN, JOAN

"I'd like to set up an audition for my wife." Phones must have been ringing off the hook at TV stations all over the country when a judge ordered "Good Morning America" anchor Joan Lunden to fork over $18,000 a month in temporary alimony to her ex-husband Michael Krause. Lunden was also ordered to pay for the mortgage, taxes, fuel, electricity, security alarms, cable television, and property insurance on the couple's Rye, New York, home, in which Krause still lives. Finally, the judge ordered Lunden to pay $25,000 to Krause's attorney and $15,000 to his accountant.

MAPLES, MARLA

The high-profile girlfriend of the higher-profile Donald Trump made headlines again when a hidden video camera caught her publicist, forty-nine-year-old Chuck Jones, allegedly sneaking into her apartment to steal shoes. After Maples filed a complaint, police allegedly found forty to fifty pairs of her shoes in Jones's apartment, as well as her bras and silk panties stuffed into drawers, air vents, and closets. According to the *New York Post,* the publicist called the paper and tearfully admitted taking the shoes.

MARCOS, IMELDA

The former Philippines first lady took some novel approaches in her campaign for the presidency of the country. First she tried appealing to the poor. At a Manila rally, she told several thousand impoverished followers, "I am a squatter, too. They took away all my properties. I am one of you." Then she climbed into her air-conditioned stretch limousine and returned to her $2,000 a day hotel suite.

Guess what—the approach didn't work. So Imelda's next tactic was to claim that the foundation of her husband's wealth was good luck—he stumbled upon a vast horde of gold hidden by the Japanese when they occupied the Philippines in World War II. Marcos further added that her late husband had generously sold much of the gold to help the Philippines through hard economic times in the 1960s and 1970s. The Philippine government countered by repeating evidence that Ferdinand Marcos accumulated his fortune through embezzlement and kickbacks.

Whatever the truth, the electorate evidently didn't have sympathy for Imelda—she lost badly.

MILKEN, MICHAEL

The former king of junk bonds, just out of jail for securities fraud, dropped from the ranks of billionaires after agreeing to pay a whopping $900 million fine to settle more than two hundred lawsuits. But don't weep for Milken—the deal leaves him with a personal fortune of $125 million and an additional

$300 million held by his wife and children. Now, don't you consider that punishment?

MONROE, MARILYN

Astonishing fascination with this actress continues three decades after her death. By the thirtieth anniversary of her demise, August 4, 1992, a total of eighty-four books about her had been published, with several more in the works.

These books contain increasingly spectacular charges. The latest, a book called *Double Cross* written by Chuck Giancana, brother of the late Chicago crime boss Sam Giancana, charges that a four-man hit team sent by the mob assassinated Monroe in hopes of exposing her romance with former Attorney General Robert Kennedy. According to Giancana, the hit team pinned the nude actress to the bed, taped her mouth, and inserted a suppository filled with Nembutal, a powerful barbiturate.

NORIEGA, MANUEL

The ex-Panamanian dictator didn't have a great year in 1992. First of all, he was sentenced to forty years in prison after his conviction on drug-related charges. And his wife, Felicidad Noriega, was arrested at a Miami, Florida, department store on charges of grand theft for ripping buttons worth $305 off of clothes hanging on the rack. She later pled guilty to a reduced charge and made restitution.

OYL, OLIVE

The long-time (very long-time) main squeeze of Popeye the Sailor strongly asserted a woman's right to choose on the abortion issue in a comic strip penned by cartoonist Bobby London, who'd been drawing the weekday episodes since 1986. But King Features, which syndicates the comic, muffled the outspoken maiden, withdrawing the sequence and firing London. Said an angry Popeye, defending his love, "That's all I can stands, I can't stands no more."

PRINCESS DIANA

The wife of the heir to the British throne spent 1992 in the eye of the biggest storm of royal gossip and scandal since King Edward VIII renounced his throne to marry American divorcee Wallis Simpson. Three best-selling books, numerous tabloid articles, and dozens of interviews with confidantes of both Princess Di and her husband Prince Charles provided a portrait of an extremely troubled marriage.

Sources close to the Princess described her as a woman so devastated by her husband's formality and aloofness that she developed bulimia and attempted suicide. Sources close to the Prince described him as a man driven away by an immature, spoiled, temperamental wife who has no appreciation of the duties and responsibilities of a future king.

Public sentiment, as expressed in British public opinion polls, was solidly on the side of Princess Di. The aristocracy rallied around the Prince. The two divorced after one of the most publicized marital battles in history.

QUAYLE, DAN

The famous "potatoe" incident isn't the only poor spelling to haunt the vice president. Patrons of golf legend Sam Snead's Tavern in Orlando, Florida, were reading memorabilia on the wall when they came across a note from Quayle to Snead that read: "Sam, had a great time this weekend but the golf was lousey." So's your spelling, Danny.

REAGAN, NANCY

In her autobiography, *The Way I See It,* Patti Davis charged that her mother, Nancy Reagan, was a child beater who to lived in a fog of tranquilizers. Davis said her mother took five or six pills daily and was prone to frequent violent rages that sometimes included physical violence. Ronald Reagan's response at the time, according to his daughter, was, "He said I was lying and he said I was crazy. I really realized I was never going to know what it would feel like to have a father."

REYNOLDS, BURT

Reynolds revealed that he had been $30 million in debt three years ago before his new hit TV show "Evening Shade" began to air. A persistent, painful infection in his jawbone led to his becoming addicted to the sleeping pill Halcion. He said his resulting inattention to his affairs led to his being wiped out financially. However, Reynolds was able to negotiate a deal with CBS that gave him fifty percent ownership of "Evening Shade" along with a hefty salary. Reynolds could receive as much as $100 million when the sitcom goes into syndication.

RIVERA, GERALDO

In one of the all-time low points of television talk show history, viewers and a live audience of 250 people watched as a cosmetic surgeon removed a needle of fat from Geraldo Rivera's buttocks and injected it into his face to smooth out wrinkles.

RIVERS, JOAN

Rivers's syndicated talk show is taped in the same Manhattan building as CBS's "60 Minutes." On June 16, 1992, Rivers received a letter from Susan Bieber, an assistant producer at "60 Minutes" which read, "It has been brought to my attention from a number of women at '60 Minutes' that your employees are allowing Spike [Rivers's dog] to urinate over the toilet bowls of the ninth-floor bathroom. We would appreciate it if your employees could walk your dog outside. I thank you."

Rivers sarcastically wrote back, "This is absolutely impossible, as everyone knows Spike urinates over the toilet bowls on the eighth floor." Charges were traded back and forth until "60 Minutes" producer Don Hewitt stepped in to bring peace to the bathrooms on West 57 Street.

SCHWARZENEGGER, ARNOLD

Readers of *Spy* Magazine recently saw all of the muscled box-office champ as they published two nude pictures taken during the early 1970s when Schwarzenegger was a body builder hustling for attention. The magazine's publisher said he was not originally planning to use the photographs, but was angered when the Terminator's publicist demanded the photos not be used.

TYSON, MIKE

Erinn Cosby, twenty-five-year-old daughter of Bill Cosby, appeared on television's "Entertainment Tonight," "Donahue," and "Night Talk with Jane Whitney" to charge that Mike Tyson had sexually assaulted her three years before. She said the incident occurred in Tyson's New Jersey mansion. According to her, Bill Cosby angrily demanded that Tyson agree to undergo psychotherapy. However, the boxer apparently reneged on his agreement to see a shrink. And look where he ended up.

Eleven

Human Nature

Great Moments in American Education

It seems to be the general consensus that education is getting worse these days. Maybe that's why educators have been reaping an unusually fine harvest of fractured English from papers submitted by college students. Following is a sample for your amusement:

* A virgin forest is a place where the hand of man has never set foot.
* Although the patient had never been fatally ill before, he woke up dead.
* Arabs wear turbines on their heads.

* It is bad manners to break your bread and roll in your soup.
* The problem with intersexual swimming is that the boys often outstrip the girls.
* A triangle which has an angle of 135 degrees is called an obscene triangle.
* The bowels are a, e, i, o, u and sometimes w and y.
* In *The Glass Menagerie,* Laura's leg keeps coming between her and other people.
* The death of Francis MaComber was a turning point in his life.
* The Gorgons had long snakes in their hair. They looked like women, only more horrible.
* The Puritans thought every event significant because it was a massage from God.
* The difference between a king and a president is that a king is the son of his father, but a president isn't.
* The three kinds of blood vessels are arteries, vanes, and caterpillars.
* A fossil is an extinct animal. The older it is, the more extinct it is.
* Artificial insemination is when the farmer does it to the cow and not the bull.
* To be a good nurse, you must be absolutely sterile.
* Rural life is lived mostly in the country.
* Heredity means that if your grandfather didn't have any children, then your father probably wouldn't have any, and neither would you, probably.
* Necessity is the mother of convention.

Finally, and most appropriately:
* The amount of education you have determines your loot in life.

Truly Weird Stories

Let's face it — perhaps the most bizarre stories in the world are created by the very weird things that ordinary, everyday people do. Here are some of those strange tales:

* A surgeon who served as chief of staff at one of the nation's most famous burn hospitals was brought up for disciplinary action by the American College of Surgeons for using a surgical marker to draw pictures on various body parts of his patients. The doodling doc allegedly put happy faces on the penises of two patients and on the upper abdomen of a third. He had previously been suspended by the hospital for a week for placing his initials on the skull of a severely burned nine-month-old infant.

* You've heard of shotgun weddings, but we'll bet you don't know that a Des Moines, Iowa, man has come up with the shotgun funeral. Specifically, he believes it's a shame for the ashes of people who loved hunting to end up in a cold urn on some mantel. So for the cost of a normal internment, he loads the hunter's ashes into shotgun shells and drives to the hunter's favorite woods, marsh, or other location. After performing whatever ritual the family requests, he loads the shells and blasts the ashes away.

While the shotgun funerals are the man's most popular service, he will also put ashes in bowling balls, baseball bats, or almost anything else. One woman sent her father's ashes to be stuffed into her golf clubs.

* A thirty-five-year-old Baltimore physician who used to work in the emergency room at Johns Hopkins Hospital was apparently furious at his ex-girlfriend — so furious that he put her name on a blood sample from an AIDS patient. You can imagine the woman's mental agony until the truth came out. The state medical board ordered the physician to perform one hundred hours of community service and apologize to the woman — but is that enough?

* There is dumb. There is dumber. Then there is a kind of stupidity beyond human comprehension. That rare level was reached by a Florida woman who suffers from asthma. So she kept an inhaler containing her asthma spray under her pillow — along with a loaded revolver.

You guessed it. One night she suffered an asthma attack. Half-asleep, she reached for what she thought was her inhaler, put it to her mouth, and pressed what she thought was the button to release the spray. Shortly afterwards she was taken to the hospital for shooting herself in the jaw.

* A Loxahatchee, Florida, company offers a unique, new home delivery service aimed at a yet unserved market — jilted lovers and other disgruntled people. For a fee, Poop-Poop We Do delivers a bouquet of cow manure to the object of the sender's wrath. One woman made a stink to the state health department after receiving a bouquet, but since cow manure is widely available at garden stores, the service appears headed for a "clean" bill of health.

* A Bloomfield, New Mexico, woman whose insurance company wouldn't pay to have her silicone breast

181

implants removed performed the surgery on herself one night after her husband and children went to bed. She took some Valium to steady herself, then slit herself with a razor. She managed to squeeze the silicone gel from the implants, but couldn't manage to remove the bags. The next day, a doctor removed the bags at his office.

The woman's husband said this wasn't her first attempt at self-surgery — she'd tried unsuccessfully to remove a wisdom tooth with a pair of pliers.

* Attention, lovers of fine art. If you're really lucky, the Fine Art Gallery at the Cheney Cowles Museum in Spokane, Washington, might schedule an encore of last winter's feature exhibit — cow skulls and road kill such as dead rabbits and a flattened coyote were on display. During the exhibit, the museum had to call in exterminators to deal with flies, beetles, and other pests that began to feed on the "art." Now, aren't you sorry you missed it?

* A woman stopped her family van at a highway rest stop in Newport, Tennessee, so her children could go to the bathroom. She took her daughters to the ladies' room, while her five-year-old son headed into the men's room. A few minutes later, she piled the kids back into the van and took off. Seventy miles down the road, she pulled into a fast-food restaurant to order lunch. It was only then she discovered she'd left her son in Newport, Tennessee.

* A Southfield, Minnesota, two-year-old tumbled out of a ninth floor apartment window and was falling to certain death eighty feet below when his diaper snagged on a bush, stopping his descent. The diaper tape finally gave way, and the infant fell a few feet to the

ground naked but virtually unhurt. We bet his new nickname is Lucky.

* A Denver, Colorado, cab driver was shot in the mouth during a robbery — and walked out of the hospital that night. What was the reason for this miracle? The bullet hit the man's dentures and fragmented, causing only minor cuts.

* Ever have one of those days when nothing goes right, no matter how hard you try? A thirty-year-old Kenmore, New York, man evidently had one of those days when he decided to kill himself by leaping out a fourth-story window. Because the building's windows don't open, the man took a running leap, smashed through the glass, fell forty feet — but landed on the top of a car that absorbed most of the impact. A little dazed but undaunted, the would-be suicide jumped up, ran into the building, took the elevator to the fourth floor, leaped out the window again — and landed on the same car. This time he broke his wrist and ankle. Police caught up with him and took him to the hospital before he could try a third time.

Fractured Headlines

Newspaper headline writers want to attract attention — but sometimes they end up getting stares for the wrong reason. Following are some hilarious headlines from the U.S. press:

* GRANDMOTHER OF EIGHT MAKES HOLE IN ONE
* DEAF MUTE GETS NEW HEARING IN KILL-

ING
* DEFENDANT'S SPEECH ENDS IN LONG SENTENCE
* DOCTOR TESTIFIES IN HORSE SUIT
* POLICE BEGAN CAMPAIGN TO RUN DOWN JAYWALKERS
* COOKIES WITH CONDOMS FAIL FAMILY TASTE TEST
* LEBENESE CHIEF LIMITS ACCESS TO PRIVATE PARTS
* TREES CAN BREAK WIND
* DEAD MAN TOLD: GET BACK TO WORK
* DROUGHT TURNS COYOTES TO WATERMELONS
* MEN RECOMMEND MORE CLUBS FOR WIVES
* TWO CONVICTS EVADE NOOSE; JURY HUNG
* MAN HELD OVER GIANT L.A. BRUSH FIRE
* FURNITURE DRIVE FOR HOMELESS LAUNCHED
* MAN SHOT, STABBED; DEATH BY NATURAL CAUSES RULED
* TRAFFIC DEAD RISE SLOWLY
* COLLEGIANS ARE TURNING TO VEGETABLES
* S. FLORIDA ILLEGAL ALIENS TO BE CUT IN HALF
* THUGS EAT THEN ROB PROPRIETOR
* NEW HOUSING FOR ELDERLY NOT YET DEAD
* BAN ON NUDE DANCING ON GOVERNOR'S DESK
* DEATH ROW INMATES NO LONGER AL-

LOWED DAY OFF AFTER EXECUTION
* WOMAN DEAD WHEN HEAD REMOVED
* *QUEEN MARY* HAVING BOTTOM SCRAPED
* WOMEN'S MOVEMENT CALLED MORE BROAD-BASED
* IDAHO GROUP ORGANIZES TO HELP SERVICE WIDOWS
* CHILD'S STOOL GREAT FOR USE IN GARDEN
* CAUSE OF AIDS FOUND — SCIENTISTS
* ORGAN FESTIVAL ENDS IN SMASHING CLIMAX
* IN THE SEWERS, EACH DAY'S JOB HAS NEW ALLURE
* CHARCOAL BRIQUETTES DESTROYED BY FIRE
* LAWMEN FROM MEXICO BARBECUE GUESTS
* MINERS REFUSE TO WORK AFTER DEATH

You're Selling What?

Most small businesses and individuals who write classified ads can't afford fancy New York ad agencies. So sometimes what appears in print is not what they intended:

* TWO DAY SALE: FRIDAY ONLY
* BRAILLE DICTIONARY FOR SALE — Must see to appreciate
* FARMER LOOKING FOR WIFE WITH TRACTOR: If interested, send picture of tractor

* LOST: Donald Duck wallet. Need for identification.
* WILL SWAP WHITE SATIN WEDDING DRESS FOR 50 POUNDS FRESH GRAVY TRAIN
* FOR SALE: Antique desk suitable for lady with thick legs and large drawers
* USED CARS: Why go elsewhere to be cheated? Come here first!
* MODULAR SOFAS: Only $299. For rest or fore play
* BABY-SITTER: Looking for infant to baby-sit in my home.
* NEED PLAIN CLOTHES SECURITY: Must have shoplifting experience
* WANTED: Man to take care of cow that does not smoke or drink
* 3-YEAR-OLD TEACHER NEEDED FOR PRE-SCHOOL
* ILLITERATE? Write today for free help.
* EARS PIERCED WHILE YOU WAIT
* FORECLOSURE LISTINGS: Entire state of New Jersey available
* DON'T KILL YOUR WIFE: Let our washing machine do the dirty work
* WONDERFUL BARGAINS FOR MEN WITH 16 AND 17 NECKS
* YES, WE ARE OPEN. Sorry for the inconvenience.

Twelve:

All About John

When Was the Bathroom Invented?

"Boy," you're probably saying, "what a dumb question! After all, people have always had to go." The need to relieve oneself is unquestioned; however, standards of hygiene haven't always been anywhere near our standards today.

Curiously, many of the great ancient civilizations put great store in cleanliness and spent a lot of time designing facilities both to eliminate waste and cleanse the body. Homes in the Indus River Valley had bathrooms as early as 3000 B.C., and noble Minoan families on Crete built homes with systems of pipes to carry off wastes by the year 2000 B.C. Egyptian aristocrats used copper piping to bring in hot and cold water and remove unwanted materials. The Romans were big on bathing, building immense and immaculate bathing facilities that the wealthy used every day. Personal hygiene and grooming were held in very high regard.

The fall of Rome also brought about the decline of hygiene. One culprit was Christianity, which taught that the flesh was evil. For centuries, the only time in their lives people bathed by immersion was when they were baptized. Since exposing their flesh was evil, no one washed. Rich people doused themselves with perfume, and poor people just stank.

At the same time, very few people paid any attention to where they relieved themselves. In the 1500s, the situation got so bad in British palaces that the royal family had to post notices warning people not to urinate and defecate in hallways, stairways, or public rooms. The great French palace at Versaille, built in the 1600s to house the French royal family, one thousand noblemen, and four thousand servants, had not one single bathroom.

In fact, the reinvention of the bathroom did not take place until the spread of another invention—the modern flush toilet. The first device was built in England in 1775 by a mathematician and watchmaker named Alexander Cunningham. His device included a backwards-shaped pipe that permanently held water and prevented cesspool fumes from backing up into the bathroom. However, it was about another one hundred years before indoor flush toilets began to make inroads replacing outhouses and chamber pots.

Who Invented Toilet Paper?

The toilet paper pioneer was an American named Joseph Gayetty, who tried to market a package of five hundred individual sheets in 1857. The venture was an outstanding failure — people couldn't understand why they had to waste good money wiping themselves when they had so many old newspapers and catalogs around. A British entrepreneur who had the idea of selling rolls of tear sheets also failed.

The breakthrough came in the 1880s when American hotels began installing indoor bathrooms. The hotels looked for something more convenient and elegant than old catalogs for the use of their guests. That need was met by two brothers named Edward and Clarence Scott, who had developed smaller, more manageable toilet paper rolls. Their initial product, which bore the prestigious name of the Waldorf Hotel, was later changed to ScotTissue.

Who Invented Kleenex?

The story of facial tissue starts in 1914 at the beginning of World War I. Cotton was in very short supply, so companies began to look for absorbent materials to use as surgical bandages and as wadding in gas masks. A company named Kimberly-Clark came up with a cotton-like substance called Cellucotton, and they began to produce it in huge quantities.

Then the war ended and Kimberly-Clark had warehouses full of the stuff. One application was as a female sanitary napkin that the company named Kotex. The other was as a wipe to remove makeup. Kimberly-Clark dubbed the wipe a Kleenex Kerchief and hired a number of Hollywood stars such as Helen Hayes and Gertrude Lawrence to promote it.

Kleenex became popular. Then Kimberly-Clark began receiving letters from women explaining (or complaining) that their husbands were using the tissues as disposable handkerchiefs. At first the company didn't like the idea, because it somehow seemed unsanitary. However, with the invention of the pop-up box in the late 1920s, that particular demand for the product became even stronger. In 1930, Kimberly-Clark finally gave in and began marketing Kleenex as a dual use product.

When Was Soap Invented?

Soap was first invented by the Phoenicians about 600 B.C. In a process known as saponification, they boiled goat fat, water, and ash which left a solid, waxy substance when totally evaporated. This substance contained two different types of molecules. The first attached itself to water molecules; the second latched on to molecules of dirt and grease. So rinse water carried away the dirt and grease. This seemingly miraculous cleaning substance was introduced to the Greeks and Romans by Phoenician traders. By the eleventh century, it was so highly prized that many governments taxed it, and people made "bootleg" soap in the dark of night. However, as bathing went out of favor, so did soap, and for centuries very little was manufactured.

Soap came back into favor in the 1800s, but users soon learned it had its limitations. Soap, when combined with certain chemicals and minerals in water, formed insoluble compounds that left a scum on bathtubs and spots on glasses. This problem was solved in Germany during World War I. Cut off from its supply of natural fats to make soap, German chemists experimented with artificial molecules that, combined with alcohol, lathered up like soap but left no traces behind. These new combinations were called detergents. Today, we use gentler soap for washing our bodies, but we use detergents on our clothes and dishes.

What Do We Do in the Bathroom?

On the average, we go to the bathroom five or six times per day. And we do a lot more than relieve ourselves. About forty percent of people read in the bathroom, twenty percent smoke, fourteen percent listen to the radio, and eight percent talk on the telephone.

Bathroom designers, in an ongoing quest to make bathrooms more comfortable, have even studied our most intimate habits. They have discovered that thirty-six percent of us flush while still sitting, while sixty-four percent stand up to flush.